MINNESOTA TWINS TRIVIA

1,069 Questions
(and answers, too!)

Jim Hoey

NODIN PRESS

ACKNOWLEDGEMENTS

I would like to thank all of the people who have supported my efforts in compiling this book and to those who gave me suggestions and counsel. To my wonderful wife Ann and my son Eddie, I thank you for accepting my passion for Twins baseball and for allowing me the time to do this project and for your love and understanding. And Ann, thanks for letting me put in my Metropolitan Stadium seats in the basement!

I want to thank Norton Stillman for his guidance and direction in publishing this book, and John Toren for the wonderful job he did editing it. I would also like to thank the Twins organization, and Molly Gallatin in particular, for allowing us to use photographs from their collection. I am humbled and honored to have had the opportunity to be involved in this endeavor. To all of you Twins fans and readers, I hope you enjoy reading the book as much as I did creating it.

ISBN: 978-1-932472-99-8
Library of Congress Control Number: 2010924718

Photographs courtesy of the Minnesota Twins, all rights reserved.
Cover art: Karl Jaeger
Design: John Toren

Nodin Press
530 North Third Street
Suite 120
Minneapolis, MN 55401

Every effort has been made to ensure the accuracy of the information contained in this book. If you notice an error please notify us and we'll correct it for the next edition. Thank you and enjoy the book!

- Jim Hoey, ajehoey@comcast.net

MINNESOTA TWINS TRIVIA

Joe Mauer

for Twins fans everywhere

CONTENTS

INTRODUCTION: BASEBALL AND ME

For more than 30 years I have been employed as a social studies teacher, but sports, especially baseball, has been a passion of mine from an early age. I also enjoy writing (I once worked a stint as a sportswriter) and have an affinity for statistics. Put those four enthusiasms together—history, statistics, writing, and baseball—and the end-result is the book you hold in your hands, a trivia and quiz book on the Minnesota Twins.

With the Twins playing ball on their new Target Field, and their 50th anniversary season on the horizon, it seemed like an appropriate time to put such a volume together. And while assembling it I've enjoyed recalling fond memories of my own passion for the sport (and the Twins) as both a child and adult. Throughout the years, I have correlated events in my life with the rhythm of Twins seasons. Many of the team's 7,807 games are indelibly etched in my mind, as are most of the 660 players who have competed for the club thus far. My hope is that readers will be able to recall specific incidents and relish memories of former players and teams as they peruse these pages.

One of my dreams as a youngster was to find work in the Twin Cities so I could go to major-league games, cheering for my home-state team. That childhood dream came true, and in the past 35 years I have been able to attend more than a thousand of them. I was raised on Minnesota's Iron Range in the village aptly called Taconite, and my earliest baseball memories were shaped by my father, Ed, who was a Detroit Tiger fan and a Lou Gehrig devotee. Over the years, he and I have watched countless games together, debating their intricacies and analyzing the strategy involved. Dad was a heckuva pitcher himself, once being offered a scholarship to the University of Virginia after a naval officer saw him pitch during WWII.

My first recollection of reading, not surprisingly, is of pouring over box scores in the Duluth *News Tribune* in the late 1950's—especially those of the team nearest us, the Milwaukee Braves. Milwaukee was a long way from the Mesabi Range, and the interstate freeway system was just a piece of legislation on Eisenhower's desk, but I learned how to spell names of standouts like Aaron, Adcock, Mathews, and Spahn, and to rattle off their statistics. While we were a town centered around hockey, we also relished our baseball.

Then in late 1960, it was announced that the Washington Senators were relocating to the Minneapolis-St. Paul area and that the Upper Midwest would have its own major-league team. In that inaugural year, 1961, I was just a third-grader, but I can vividly recall the palpable excitement during that first spring. At the age of 8, I was thrilled when Pedro Ramos shut out the defending world champion Yankees 6-0 in their first game as the Minnesota Twins and at historic Yankee Stadium, to boot.

My paternal grandfather, Ambrose Hoey, was finishing up his career with the Cleveland-Cliffs Iron Company and lived with our burgeoning family, which now totaled five boys and two girls and was well on its way to a total of eight and two. Grandpa owned a maroon Zenith radio, and from his second-floor bedroom I listened to late-night games broadcast by KOZY out of Grand Rapids. When I had to go to sleep in an adjacent bedroom, I would sometimes lay down outside his door with my ear to the floor to catch the scratchy broadcast.

While some of my friends and family gravitated toward the more traditional North Woods pursuits of fishing and hunting, I became fixated on baseball, and specifically, the Twins franchise. They had been routinely one of the American League's worst teams during their final decades in Washington, but once in Minnesota, the organization assembled a group of young players headed by sluggers Harmon Killebrew and Bob Allison, pitchers Camilo Pascual and Jim Kaat, and an exciting shortstop named Zoilo Versalles. There was no question that this was a team with talent, potential, and flair.

The sights and sounds of the Twins were everywhere prior to that first season in Minnesota. Schedules were posted around town and the sound of the flagship station, WCCO, could be heard as easily as the big Euclid trucks and railroad cars unloading and loading iron ore. How about those Hamms beer radio advertisements and television commercials! Many a night I went to sleep listening to the voices of Ray Scott, Bob Wolff, and Halsey Hall just imagining being at Metropolitan Stadium in person. (Remember, Herb Carneal didn't join the staff until 1962.)

Rising each morning meant a race downstairs to read the box scores from the previous day. It was a chance to relive a Twins win or to wallow in a late-inning defeat. The Twins languished in ninth-place that first summer, but frequent Killebrew homers and Pascual strikeouts more than made up for their struggles, and now we had our own major-league team. And 1961 was shaping up to be an amazing year on another count: two Yankee teammates, my first idol Mickey Mantle and Hibbing-born Roger Maris, were locked in a home-run battle that might send one (or both!) of them beyond Babe Ruth's single-season home-run record of 60.

In those days, the few Twins games that were televised (mostly road games) were prized time-slots, leading to heated disputes with my two sisters over whether Frankie Avalon and Annette Funichello were more of a priority than Harmon Killebrew and Camilo Pascual. Like most families in those days, we had a single black-and-white television set, a grainy Setchell-Carlson that often required the services of our friendly repairman Clem Gallant, typically right in the midst of a game.

Seeing the Twins on TV only heightened my desire to see them in person, and finally, a few years after they arrived in the Twin Cities, an opportunity presented itself. As one of the altar boys for our parish, I was part of a larger group, sponsored by the local chapter of the Knights of Columbus, that made the journey by bus to the 'Cities to watch a Twins game on a Saturday morning as part of a "knothole gang." We were also privileged to take in a baseball clinic sponsored by the Twins prior to the game.

Matters of baseball aside, that trip to the city was exciting from beginning for end to a ten-year-old kid who had seldom left his village. The towns we passed on the way down were interesting, and the once we reached the metropolis of Minneapolis, we got to see buildings more than three stories high and a lot of classic cars, too, even if they weren't classics just yet. There were plenty of hijinks on the bus, as you would expect with a busload of kids aged 8 to 13. We left at 5 a.m. for the five-hour, 210 mile trip. And on top of all of that, there would be baseball, Twins baseball! I would be seeing a real major-league game before we headed back to the Iron Range later that day. I would have my glove ready to catch a Killebrew drive in the left field bleachers.

That summer, the Twins were challenging the world champion Yankees in the eight-team American League and would eventually finish in second-place, just five games behind Mantle, Maris, Berra, Ford, and the rest of that stellar team. Dick Stigman, a lefty who was one of us—a Minnesotan from Nimrod—was on the mound that day. Would we win? If we did, I would get up early on the next morning to scour the famous sports "peach" section of the *Minneapolis Star-Tribune*, which would have a big article and lots of pictures. We might even spot ourselves sitting in the stands!

We were all awed by the vastness and the traffic of the metro area, and once we'd reached the outskirts it still seemed to take forever to get to the ballpark. Suddenly, somebody yelled out that they saw a road sign for Bloomington and asked if that was where the Twins played. I screamed out, "Yes"! We knelt on the seats to peer out the windows.

Finally, we could see the light towers of Metropolitan Stadium and the huge parking lot signs with the names of all the American League teams. Like freed captives, we scrambled off the bus into the warmth of a cloudless July morning. Straight ahead, we could see the colored brick that adorned the outside of the main structure, but we headed to the left-field stands where we would watch Angelo Guiliani and his cohorts lead the instructional clinic.

My heart was pounding as our group proceeded through the turnstiles. In the distance I could see the third deck of the grandstand, and hustling forward in my PF Flyers, I caught sight of the green expanse of the field. I stopped just to feast my eyes on it and relish the moment.

From that moment on, everything took on a heightened interest, from the baseball instruction in the clinic and batting practice to infield and outfield practice. It was a whirlwind of sensations. I found the three hours prior to game just as exciting as the game itself. In fact, I was so busy observing everything I almost forgot to eat. Though Dad had given me $10 to spend on food and memorabilia, once the game started I didn't miss a pitch. It was all good, all of it. The Twins won and we trudged back to our bus, happy even though we knew we wouldn't get home until after dark.

Back in Taconite, where I was related to half the town's 350 residents, there was some sort of athletic contest every day. We played real baseball for six weeks in our local recreational league during the summer; the ballfield was right next to the Holman mine, and sliding into any base would give you a unique red stain from the iron ore right under the playing surface. We played other "ball" games depending on how many guys we had and what space was available. We played "rubber ball" in our old tennis court opposite-handed, and softball in the outdoor hockey rink where anything not hit to straightaway center was an out. The local mine office provided a great spot for playing "wiffle-ball," and at the local elementary school we could play whatever we wanted—the size of the sphere didn't matter. We made up our own rules and played as long as we felt like it. At our house, we ate dinner at 5 p.m., but I often lingered for one final at-bat, fully aware that I'd have to do all the dishes as punishment for the chance to get another right handed rip at bat.

My playing companions had names like Squeeky, Cotton, Trikey, Looney, Cool Jerk, and Peanuts, just to name a few. And if you were good enough, you got to play against the older kids like Quincy,

Sluggo, and Johnny X, and really advance your game. It was a wonderful place to grow up—almost idyllic—because you had the freedom and opportunity to be creative and just be a kid. It was all remindful of that wonderful flick *The Sandlot*, except that nobody made the major leagues and nobody faked their impending drowning to get mouth-to-mouth from the best-looking lifeguard at the beach.

As we weaved our way into becoming teenagers, other pursuits found their way into our lives. The usual dalliances—girls and cars—became paramount for most but not for me. While I did become familiar with the other gender, baseball had a peculiar hold on me, and I sometimes wondered if I would ever grow out of the "baseball" thing. I didn't.

The Twins won the A.L. pennant in 1965 and took on the Los Angeles in the Series, a team with great pitching and speed. I was in the eighth grade. We jumped ahead 2-0 but then lost three straight out in Los Angeles. I remember listening to game 6 over the public-address system in Bugsy Bogdanovich's shop class, and hearing the crowd roar when "Mudcat" Grant slammed a three-run homer to help us tie the series at 3-3. But the next day, Koufax shut us out 2-0 in the decisive seventh game. The devastation was deep. I couldn't read the newspapers for two weeks and even watching Fran Tarkenton's scrambling couldn't make up for that heart-rending defeat.

In 1967, the Hoey boys watched Carl Yazstremski break our hearts with his heroics at Fenway to end the season with two straight over the Twins. More heartbreak. On a positive note, one of my girlfriends loved baseball and the Twins, especially Killebrew. She sent him cakes on his birthday (June 29) and probably still does. As a senior in high school and as a freshman in college, I witnessed the Baltimore Orioles demolish the Twins 3-0 in the first two American League championship series. The next year, Tony Oliva hurt his knee and was never the same. Curses! The Twins went into a funk for much of the 1970's. A college girlfriend even had the same birthday (April 6) as my favorite player, Bert Blyleven.

ONCE I'D GRADUATED from college, the Twin Cities became my home, and I worked various odd jobs to scrape together enough money to buy seats in the left-field bleachers. No matter, as Rod Carew's artistry with the bat was evident from anywhere in the stands. I was there on the day in 1977 when Sir Rodney raised his average to .403 in a truly memorable game against the White Sox. In a stretch of ten days in June, while working at a nursing home as an orderly, I was able to watch the Twins every day against Texas, Chicago, and Milwaukee in spectacular weather. My $2.65-an-hour job paid for enough gas for my '66 Dodge Coronet to make it back and forth to Bloomington and keep my radio stocked with batteries. Eating became optional but a subscription to both the *St. Paul Pioneer Press* and the *Minneapolis Star Tribune* was a necessity.

In the fall of 1977 I began my full-time teaching and coaching career, which allowed me to attend games more often and secure better seats on occasion. No matter that Hosken Powell and Bombo Rivera manned the outfield, it was still major-league baseball, and John Castino and Jerry Koosman were fun to watch.

On a gloomy and bleak day, Sept. 30, 1981, a colleague covered my last-period class at Farmington High and I made a frantic dash north to the familiar edifice just east of Cedar Avenue to see at least a part of the final game at Metropolitan Stadium. As I rushed into the stadium the scoreboard indicated we were trailing Kansas City in the bottom of the fifth inning. It seemed surreal. Standing just above me as the game ended, a 5-2 loss to the Royals, was owner Calvin Griffith. He was in his trench coat with a fedora on his head and his hands in his pockets; you could see how tough it was for him to see it all end. Fans rushed onto the field to secure some of the grass and dirt while others went to work with whatever tools they had smuggled in to dismantle seats and other souvenirs. Security guards were everywhere, as the Vikings were yet to finish their season, but thievery was still widespread.

One step inside Hubert Horatio Humphrey Stadium in downtown Minneapolis the next April was enough to confirm the reports—the structure was obviously no baseball park. Yet the big blue, green, and white excuse for a ball field nevertheless did serve as the location for some amazing moments. At least we still had our team. And after a few shaky years, during which many talented young players earned their stripes, we were all gifted with that first World Series title in 1987 with the magnificent "Cube", Kirby Puckett, and his cohorts Kent Hrbek, Gary Gaetti, Frank Viola, and Bert Blyleven. The madhouse downtown that Sunday evening after the 4-2 win in Game 7 over St. Louis remains one of the highlights of my life.

I met my future wife Ann on September 30, 1989, the second-to-last day of the season, when Seattle downed the Twins 2-1. Thus baseball hardly interfered with our "wooing" season, and we got engaged a couple months later and wed on July 7 (Yankees 5-4 over Twins) in the suburb where former Twin (and friend) Craig Kusick coached high school ball. We took a three-week honeymoon out to New England. Part of the agreement to go out to the Northeast was to witness a game at Fenway Park. As luck would have it, the Twins were playing there in mid-July and we ordered tickets for July 17. We drove in from our "love-nest" in southern Vermont and then took the subway to the venerable old ballpark. We sat down near the "Pesky Pole" in foul territory and enjoyed a pitchers' duel between Boston's Tom Bolton and our own Scott Erickson.

If this wasn't nirvana, it was close, what with the love of your life on your arm and watching your favorite team in one of the truly great venues in sport.

Ericson found himself in a bases-loaded jam with nobody out in the fifth. Up steps former Twin Tom Brunansky. "Bruno" hits a sharp grounder to Gary Gaetti at third. Gaetti steps on third to force a runner, guns a throw to A.L. Newman at second to force another, and then Newman relays a throw to Kent Hrbek at first to easily beat Brunansky. Triple play!

In the eighth, Boston is nursing a 1-0 lead and reliever John Candelaria quickly finds himself in the same bases-loaded, no-out situation. Jody Reed is at the plate and he raps another sharp grounder to Gaetti, who is again close to the bag at third. He replicates his earlier actions and so do both Newman and Hrbek. Reed is out by a step.

Triple play! The crowd gasps and I leap to my feet to applaud.

My bride pulls on my arm and asks, "Does this happen very often."

"Well, uh, no," I replied. "It has never happened, ever, in the entire history of the game."

For our first Valentines Day in 1991, Ann presented me with a handsome frame and the two tickets stubs from that memorable game inside. The tickets were signed with the names…Gary Gaetti, Al Newman, and Kent Hrbek…in blue ink. It is one of my most cherished mementos. Love and baseball, all intertwined. Later in '91, we rejoiced in a second World Series title!

In 2000, the Twins sponsored an essay contest to name their all-time fan over their first 40 years. I was one of ten finalists for that lofty award, though it was eventually awarded to an 18-year old kid who hadn't even been alive for more than half of the Twins' games. Manager Tom Kelly, grumpy as ever, actually picked the winner out of a hat. It should have gone to the 83-year-old lady who had only missed a handful of games. On the night the award was given out, I got to stand next to Jacque Jones in left-field during the national anthem—long enough to remind him to lay off the high fastball and the curve a foot wide of the plate.

With the resurrection of the Twins under Ron Gardenhire, I attended several playoff games with my young son, Eddie, who correctly predicted the score in a 2-1 win over the Angels in Game 1 of the 2002 A.L. championship series. Unfortunately, he picked us to win 22-1 the next day, and we ended up losing 6-3, and lost the series 4-1. So much for soothsaying! Though the club has made five forays into the playoffs since 2002, they haven't had much post-season success. However, a new generation of Twins fans has been invigorated by a strong nucleus of young stars and the promise of playing on real terra firma under the real sky. The Twins have been good and exciting in the first decade of the 21st century and now they are assured of playing in this market for the next 30 years in a real baseball park.

With two of baseball's best players (Joe Mauer and Justin Morneau) in our lineup for the next decade, it's time for optimism. Let's hope that the Twins can build around them and bring a third World Series title to the Twin Cities. We've had a World Series played at both of the Twins previous venues, and perhaps it won't be long before we're watching one in Target Field.

MINNESOTA TWINS TRIVIA

Camilo Pascual

1

THE INAUGURAL SEASON OF 1961

1) The Twins played their first game as a Minnesota-based franchise after relocating from Washington, D.C. on April 11, 1961. What team did they face in that historic opener and what was the result?

2) On June 6, 1961, after the Twins had lost 16 of 17 games, manager "Cookie" Lavagetto was replaced by a Twins coach. Who was he?

3) What was the total attendance at Metropolitan Stadium in Bloomington that year?

4) What Twins righthander led the American League in strikeouts in 1961, and what was his total?

5) What Twins pitcher tied Baltimore's Steve Barber for the A.L. lead in shutouts with 8, despite posting a losing record (15-16)?

6) What number did shortstop Zoilo Versalles, the first Twin to come to bat for the team, wear during his Minnesota career?

7) What three broadcasters were on the Twins flagship radio broadcast crew?

8) In 1961 the starting centerfielder for the Twins put together a 24-game hitting streak—a record that stood for 18 years. What was his name?

9) In their first year the Twins' four starting pitchers all pitched 200 innings or more (a feat only duplicated once, in 1967). Who were they?

10) What was the starting lineup and their defensive positions when the Twins took the field for the first time?

11) What Twins pitcher hurled back-to-back shutouts on three occasions in 1961?

12) Who was the first Twins hitter to record five hits in a game?

13) What future Twins coach and manager was the starting second baseman in the Twins' first game?

14) Who was the first native-Minnesotan to appear in a game for the Twins?

15) What Twins pitcher pitched a shutout over the world-champion Yankees in the team's first-ever game in Yankee Stadium?

16) What team did the Twins face in their first-ever game at Metropolitan Stadium on April 21, 1961, and what was the result?

17) Who was the first Twins player to homer in front of the home-town fans at Met Stadium?

18) Which Twins batter recorded the historic first hit for the team and who was the opposing pitcher?

19) Which player was the first to steal a base for the Twins?

21) What Twins outfielder was charged with the team's first error? (Hint: he later became a coach with the team.)

22) In 1961, what Twins starter threw a string of six consecutive complete games?

23) Which Twins outfielder (the league's Rookie of the Year two years earlier when the team was still in Washington, D.C.) hit the first homer for the Twins?

24) What Twins batter hit the first grand slam at Met Stadium?

25) Who was the primary backup at catcher for Minnesota behind regular Earl Battey in 1961?

1) New York Yankees. The Twins won 6-0 at Yankee Stadium.

2) Sam Mele

3) 1,256,723

4) Camilo Pascual with 221 strikeouts.

5) Camilo Pascual. The hard-luck pitcher fashioned a 3.46 ERA but toed the mound on the wrong days for the power-laden club.

6) Two

7) Halsey Hall, Ray Scott, and Bob Wolff. Herb Carneal joined the broadcasts in 1962.

8) Lenny Green. The lithe outfielder hit .285 and had 17 stolen bases.

9) Pedro Ramos (264 ⅓), Camilo Pascual (252 ⅓), Jack Kralick (242), and Jim Kaat (200 ⅔). In 1967, it was Dean Chance (282 ⅔), Kaat (263 ⅓), Jim Merritt (227 ⅔), and Dave Boswell (222 ⅔).

10) The starting line-up that day was:

Zoilo Versalles (SS)

Lenny Green (CF)

Harmon Killebrew (1B)

Jim Lemon (LF)

Bob Allison (RF)

Earl Battey (C)

Reno Bertoia (3B)

Billy Gardner (2B)

Pedro Ramos (P)

11) Camilo Pascual. The Havana native would lead or tie for the lead in A.L. shutouts three times in his career (1959, 1961, and 1962).

12) Zoilo Versalles

13) Billy Gardiner, who managed the Twins from 1981 to 1985.

14) Paul Giel. The former Gopher football All-American was later traded with infielder Reno Bertoia to Kansas City for outfielder Bill Tuttle before the season was half over (June 1). Giel pitched in just 12 games and was hit hard, allowing six homers and 21 runs in 19 innings.

15) Pedro Ramos, who started 34 games in '61.

16) Washington Senators. After losing the original Senators to the Twin Cities, the A.L. awarded the D.C. area an expansion team, which was also called the Senators. The "new" Senators won 5-3 in front of 24,606 fans in 63-degree temperatures. The franchise is now the Texas Rangers.

17) Don Mincher. The Alabama native would eventually hit 90 homers for the Twins from 1961-66.

18) Harmon Killebrew. The "Killer" had a single off future Hall of Famer Whitey Ford in the 4th inning in the first-ever game on April 11, 1961. Ford won the Cy Young award that season.

19) Zoilo Versalles. The flashy shortstop swiped second-base in the ninth inning of the first Twins game.

21) Jim Lemon, who made the miscue in the very first game at Yankee Stadium on April 11, 1961. The starting leftfielder made 12 errors in 120 games in the field for the Twins but countered that negative with 14 homers.

22) Camilo Pascual. Thus, six of Camilo's 15 complete games that season came in succession.

23) Bob Allison. Bob's solo shot in the 7th inning came off of Whitey Ford. An inning later, Reno Bertoia hit a two-run shot off Ford.

24) Danny Dobbek. Dobbek hit just .168 and had just four homers and 14 RBI in 72 games in his only season with the club.

25) Hal Naragon. Hal hit an impressive .302 in 139 at-bats in 57 games in the inaugural year; however, he slumped to .229 in '62.

2

THE 1960s

1) How many games did the Twins finish behind the world champion Yankees in 1962, their second year in Minnesota?

2) In 1963, the Twins clubbed the second-most homers in major-league history to that point. How many did they hit?

3) What Twins player led the A.L. in homers for three straight seasons in 1962, 1963, and 1964?

4) When the Twins won the American League pennant in 1965, they became only the third team besides New York to win the title since 1946. Who were the other two teams?

5) In 1966, the Twins (89-73) finished second behind Baltimore and only two Twins regulars hit over .260. Who were they?

6) What Twins pitcher injured his arm in the final series at Boston to decide the A.L. title in 1967 and didn't return until May of 1968?

7) Who replaced Sam Mele as Twins manager in the midst of the 1967 season?

8) In what year did the Twins have two 20-game winners with Dave Boswell (20-12) and Jim Perry (20-6)?

9) What first-baseman arrived via trade on the Twins roster a week prior to the start of the 1962 season and went on to win a Gold Glove award for his flashy play?

10) What Twins rookie outfielder belted 33 homers in 1963?

11) What Twins hitter set a league record for rookies in both hits (217) and total bases (374) in 1964?

12) When Zoilo Versalles was the A.L. M.V.P. in 1965, which of the following did he accomplish: hit over .300, knock in 100 runs, or hit 20 homers?

13) What Twins pitcher led the A.L. in wins with 25 in 1966, including eight straight in one stretch, and yet didn't win the Cy Young Award?

14) When the Twins lost the final two games of the 1967 regular season at Boston to allow the Red Sox to win the title by one game, what other team tied the Twins for second-place?

15) What specific All-Star game injury limited Harmon Killebrew to 100 games with only 17 homers and 40 runs-batted-in in 1968?

16) What Twins reliever led the A.L. in saves with 31 in 1969?

17) In 1962, the Twins rookie second baseman hit .269 with 12 homers. He had been an All-American shortstop with Purdue University the previous year. Who was he?

18) Who was the first Twins catcher to hit more than 20 homers in a season?

19) What Twins reliever became a sensation during the summer of 1963, when he recorded a sterling 1.99 earned-run-average and a 6-3 record in 66 appearances and 108⅔ innings?

20) In June of 1966, what Twins third basemen (who wore horn-rimmed glasses) was one of five Minnesota batters to homer against Kansas City in one inning along with Zoilo Versalles, Tony Oliva, Harmon Killebrew, and Don Mincher?

21) What Cuban-born Twins leftfielder, who played 108 games in 1965, mostly in left field, batted left-handed and threw left-handed and was just 5'8"?

22) What three players made up the primary outfield trio in 1968?

23) Which Twins first-baseman hit. 322 in 1969, just 10 points behind teammate Rod Carew's league-leading average?

24) When Catfish Hunter threw his perfect game against the Twins on May 8, 1968, who did he strike out on a 3-2 pitch to complete it?

25) Harmon Killebrew missed 48 games during the Twins pennant-winning year of 1965 when he dislocated his left elbow while fielding a wide throw from third-baseman Rich Rollins. Who was the Oriole baserunner who collided with Harmon on that play?

26) Who is the youngest player to ever play for the Twins?

27) What two Twins sluggers each hit grand slams in the first inning of a 14-3 win over Cleveland on July 18, 1962?

28) When the Twins won the A.L. pennant in 1965, what team finished second and how many games out did they finish?

29) What Cleveland pitcher was traded to Minnesota on May 2, 1963, in exchange for lefty starter Jack Kralick?

30) How many straight seasons did Twins slugger Harmon Killebrew swat at least 45 homers?

31) Who is the only player to ever lead his league in batting average his first two seasons?

32) In December 1964, the Twins traded pitcher Gerry Arrigo to Cincinnati for an infielder/outfielder who became one of the most popular and versatile players in Twins history? Who was he?

33) Rod Carew, the Twins infielder who used his bat like a magic wand to spray hits all around the field, was born in what country?

34) What Twins player became the second to win the Most Valuable Player award in 1969 when he slammed 49 homers and totaled a career-high 140 runs-batted-in, both league highs?

35) In 1968, when the Twins struggled mightily at the plate with a .237 team batting average, who was the primary shortstop who hit a paltry .176?

36) In which category did Harmon Killebrew lead the A.L. more often: walks or strikeouts?

37) How many times did Harmon Killebrew lead the A.L. in home-run percentage for the Twins?

38) What Twins fielder led the A.L. in errors at his position for three straight seasons during the 1960's?

39) What Twins hitter once finished fifth in the A.L. batting race despite posting an average of just .283?

40) What slick-fielding shortstop, obtained in a trade for Jim Merritt with Cincinnati, led the A.L. in putouts, assists, double plays, and total chances in 1969?

41) What Twins pitcher led the league in 1965 in wins (21), shutouts (6), and winning percentage (.750)?

42) What two Twins infielders tied for the A.L. lead in triples in 1964 with ten?

43) What Twins player led the A.L. in runs scored with less than 100 in 1963?

44) How many times did Twins outfielder Tony Oliva lead the league in hits?

45) What Twins hurler won 20 games in '62 and '63 and also led or tied the league both years in complete games with 18?

46) What Twins pitcher, who remains the club's all-time leader in wins, games started, and innings pitched, started at least 27 games for 11 straight seasons between 1961 and 1971?

47) What pitcher has the lowest career earned-run-average among Twins starters (minimum 400 innings pitched)?

48) In 1964, six Twins totaled at least 20 home runs; Harmon Killebrew led with a league-high 49, but who were the other five?

49) What pitcher logged the most innings pitched in a single outing for the Twins in the 1960's?

50) What batter (not surprisingly, a pitcher) holds the unenviable record for the worst batting average as a Twins hitter (minimum 100 at-bats)?

51) What Twins pitcher led the league in strikeouts in his first three seasons in Minnesota?

52) What Twins pitcher holds the team record for most-consecutive strikeouts?

53) The top winning percentage against any opponent in any year (15 games minimum) came in 1965, when the Twins went 17-1 against what team?

54) After Harmon Killebrew belted his 520-foot homer into the upper deck at Met Stadium in June of 1967, what did the field crew do with the seat?

55) Who became the first position player to pitch for the Twins and remains the only non-pitcher to throw more than one inning in an outing?

56) What Twins slugger is tied for the major-league record with five strikeouts in a regulation nine-inning game at Detroit on Sept. 2, 1965?

57) What Twins player holds the American League record for playing in the most games in a season with 164 in 1967?

58) Who is the only Twins pitcher to lose 20 games in a season?

59) On May 2, 1967 when the Twins hosted the Yankees, they set a record for the coldest temperature at the start of any game at Met Stadium. How cold was it?

60) What Twins lefthander tossed the first no-hitter for Minnesota?

1) 5. The Yanks' were 96-66 and the Twins were 91-71.

2) 225. Killebrew had 45, Allison, 35 and Jimmie Hall 33.

3) Harmon Killebrew in 1962 (48), 1963 (45), and 1964 (49).

4) Cleveland (1948 and 1954) and Chicago (1959)

5) Tony Oliva (.307) and Harmon Killebrew (.281)

6) Jim Kaat. On Sept. 30, with the Twins holding a one-game lead over Boston heading into the final two games at Fenway, Kaat blew out his elbow in the third inning.

7) Cal Ermer. Cal went 66-46 after taking over for Mele. The Twins finished the season one game behind Boston.

8) 1969

9) Vic Power. The Cuban native and crowd favorite, noted for gloving pop-ups with one hand, won another in '63.

10) Jimmie Hall. The outfielder never hit more than 25 his final three seasons with the Twins.

11) Tony Oliva. Despite an impressive career, Tony-O would never equal most of the hitting marks he set in his rookie season.

12) Versalles didn't do any of those; he hit .273, knocked in 77 runs, and hit 19 homers.

13) Jim Kaat. Sandy Koufax won 27 games in the N.L. and copped the Cy Young, which was awarded to just one pitcher in the majors. The following year, 1967, awards were given to the top pitcher in each league.

14) Detroit. Boston finished 92-70 with the Twins and Tigers' tied at 91-71.

15) A ruptured left hamstring; Harmon stretched for a low throw in the dirt at the Astrodome in Houston and didn't return until mid-September.

16) Ron Perranoski. The lefty had 119 ⅔ innings pitched in just 75 outings, an indication that closers often went more just the ninth inning during that era.

17) Bernie Allen. The two-sport star from Purdue was also the quarterback when the Boilermakers gave the national champion Gophers their only regular-season football defeat in 1960.

18) Earl Battey. Earl cracked out 26 in 1963 and Joe Mauer hit 28 in 2009 to break his mark.

19) Bill Dailey. Dailey, a real fan-favorite, strolled to the mound as the organist played "Won't You Come Home Bill Dailey", a play on the tune, "Won't You Come Home Bill Bailey."

20) Rich Rollins. Called "Red" because of his hair-color, Rollins was the team's starting third-baseman for over five seasons.

21) Sandy Valdespino. The diminuitive Valdespino hit .261 in '65 but slumped to .176 and .165 the next two seasons.

22) LF – Bob Allison; CF – Ted Uhlaender; RF – Tony Oliva

23) Rich Reese. He never hit above .261 during his other six full seasons with the team.

24) Rich Reese. The Twins first baseman fouled off four pitches against the 22-year-old Hunter before striking out looking on the full count. Catfish also drove in three of Oakland's runs in the 4-0 win.

25) Russ Snyder

26) Jim Manning. The Michigan native pitched in five games in April and May of 1962 as an 18-year-old. He was born on July 21, 1943 and pitched his first game on April 15, 1962. He logged just seven innings in those five appearances and his final major-league appearance was on May 2 of that year.

27) Harmon Killebrew and Bob Allison.

28) Chicago (7 games out)

29) Jim Perry. The righthander went on to pitch 10 seasons for the Twins with a 128-90 record from 1963-72 and is in the top ten in several team pitching categories.

30) Four. Killebrew hit 46 in '61, 48 in '62, 45 in '63, and 49 in '64.

31) Tony Oliva. The Cuban-born outfielder hit .323 and 321, respectively, in 1964 and 1965.

32) Cesar Tovar. The scrappy utility man played eight seasons with Minnesota and was an extremely valuable, durable and popular player. Tovar still ranks third all-time in stolen bases (168), ninth in hits (1,164), and tied for ninth in runs scored (646).

33) Panama. Carew was born on Oct. 1, 1945, in Gatun.

34) Harmon Killebrew

35) Jackie Hernandez. He had just 35 hits in 199 at-bats.

36) Bases on balls. Harmon led the A.L. four times in walks but just once in strikeouts (142 in 1962). He walked 145 times in 1969.

37) Six. Harmon also led once while with the Senators for a total of 7.

38) Zoilo Versalles. The Twin shortstop had 39 in '65, 35 in '66, and 30 in '67. Zoilo also had 30 errors in '63 and 31 in '64.

39) Ted Uhlaender. Carl Yastrzemski hit .301 to lead the league, the lowest in major-league history. Tony Oliva was third at .289.

40) Leo Cardenas. The Cuban infielder also hit .280 with 10 homers.

41) Jim "Mudcat" Grant

42) Rich Rollins and Zoilo Versalles

43) Bob Allison. The athletic leftfielder had just 99 runs scored.

44) Five. Oliva had the most hits in 1964 (217), 1965 (185), 1966 (191), 1969 (197), and 1970 (204).

45) Camilo Pascual

46) Jim Kaat. "Kitty" leads with 189 wins, 422 games started, and 2,959⅓ innings pitched.

47) Dean Chance (2.67).

48) Tony Oliva (32), Bob Allison (32), Jimmie Hall (25), Don Mincher (23) and Zoilo Versalles (20).

49) Jim Merritt. The lefty pitched 13 innings in a game in 1967.

50) Dean Chance. A right-handed batter, Chance batted .043 for the Twins as he registered just nine hits (all singles in 209 at-bats)

51) Camilo Pascual. The Cuban righthander led in 1961 (221), 1962 (206), and 1963 (202).

52) Jim Merritt (7)

53) Boston Red Sox

54) They put a baseball-shaped plaque on the seat, affirming Killebrew's feat with the date and length of the home-run. The seat was painted red. The spot where it was located, including its elevation, is now recognized at the Mall of America in Bloomington.

55) Julio Becquer. The third-baseman pitched 1 1/3 innings against Kansas City on Sept. 9, 1961 and gave up three earned runs.

56) Bob Allison.

57) Cesar Tovar.

58) Pedro Ramos (1961). Ramos had a 3.95 ERA and a 11-20 record.

59) 32 degrees (with a 17 mile-per-hour wind) as the Twins beat the Yanks 13-4. The warmest temperature ever came on June 29, 1970 when the Twins beat Kansas City 5-4 when it was 97 degrees.

60) Jack Kralick. The Ohio native no-hit the Kansas City Athletics on Aug. 26, 1962, at Met Stadium. Kralick was 67-65 in his career with an ERA of 3.56 and was traded to Cleveland for Jim Perry in 1963. The only batter to reach was George Alusik, who walked with one out in the ninth inning.

Bert Blyleven

3

THE 1970s

1) What teams did manager Bill Rigney manage before taking over for the Twins at the beginning of the 1970 season?

2) After 10 straight seasons of attendance of at least one million, in what year did the Twins dip to 940,858?

3) What Twins pitcher became the league's winningest-active pitcher when he notched his 180th win during the 1972 season?

4) In 1973, Tony Oliva became the first major-league player to do what?

5) On July 4, 1973 a capacity crowd of 45,890 at Met Stadium was present to witness the debut of what highly-touted pitcher who had just been drafted out of Arizona State, where he had a 40-4 record with a 1.64 ERA?

6) When he won his fourth straight batting crown in 1975 (with a .359 average) Rod Carew became the first hitter to win more than three in a row since what legendary hitter?

7) In 1976, Rod Carew came within three points of winning a fifth straight batting title. However, his .331 average fell just short of what two Kansas City Royal hitters?

8) What 20-year-old from Alexandria, Minnesota, was brought up in 1977 to pitch after being signed earlier at a Twins tryout camp?

9) What Twins reliever and St. Paul native went 16-7 with 15 saves in 1977 while pitching 146-⅔ innings?

10) What Twins reliever averaged more than two innings of relief per appearance in 1976, pitching 167-⅔ innings in 78 appearances while leading the A.L. in relief wins (17) and recording an ERA of 3.01?

11) With Twins pitching in a shambles in 1977, what Twins pitching coach was added to the roster at the end of the season?

12) Who holds the Twins record for innings pitched in a season with 325 in 1973?

13) During the bicentennial year of 1976, the Twins had a power outage and hit the least homers in franchise history (not counting strike years). How many homers did they hit?

14) In 1979, the Twins traded a minor-league pitcher for New York Met lefthander Jerry Koosman. Who was this minor-leaguer? (Hint: he went on to become one of the top relievers in history and pitched for the Twins in his final season.)

15) What year was the final season in Minnesota for beloved slugger Harmon Killebrew?

16) When owner Calvin Griffth uttered in a Twins commercial in the mid-to-late 1970's, "I really like that kid", what Twins player was he referring to?

17) What right-handed reliever, who appeared in 90 games in 1979 and was nicknamed, "Iron Mike", led the league with 32 saves and posted an ERA of 2.64?

18) On May 20, 1970 what hitter became the first Minnesota Twins batter to hit for the cycle?

19) How many more hits would Rod Carew have needed to hit .400 (with the same number of at-bats) when he led the majors with a .388 average in 1977, the highest since Ted Williams hit .388 in 1957?

20) As every fan knows (or should know, because Bert himself reminds TV listeners often enough) on what month and day was Bert Blyleven born in Zeist, Holland (Netherlands) in 1951?

21) Who became the Twins manager on November 24, 1975 and managed the team for four-plus seasons?

22) What was Tony Oliva's career pinch-hitting average?

23) What Twins outfielder, acquired for Paul Ray Powell from the Dodgers, slugged 22 home runs in 1972 after making his first stints in the majors with the Dodgers' as a pitcher in 1962 and 1969?

24) What Twins right-handed starter had a .500 record for three straight seasons in the '70's?

25) Who did the Twins receive in exchange for pitcher Wayne Granger in a trade in November 1972?

26) Who became the highest-paid Twin, to that point, in 1978?

27) What Twin shared the 1979 A.L. Rooke-of-the-Year award with Toronto shortstop Alfredo Griffin?

28) Who was voted the 1979 A.L. Comeback Player of the Year award after logging a 20-13 record and a 3.38 ERA?

29) What Twins designated hitter and pinch-hitter extraordinaire led the A.L. in pinch-hit appearances in 1978 (46) and 1979 (42) and led the league in pinch-hits twice (1978 and 1980)?

30) In his major-league debut as a 19-year old, Bert Blyleven beat what team 2-1 on June 5, 1970?

31) What Twins rookie started his career in 1976 as a 20-year-old catcher, hitting .260 with 10 homers and 69 RBIs and earning an All-Star berth?

32) Who was the only Twins player other than Harmon Killebrew to hit a home run into the upper deck at Met Stadium?

33) What was Rod Carew's career batting average with the Twins?

34) In the 1970's, the Twins had two outfielders on the same roster with the initials S.B. Who were they?

35) Who were the only four Twins pitchers to win 20 games in a season in the 1970's?

36) Following the 1977 season, the Twins lost two key players to free agency; one to Milwaukee and one to California. Who were they?

37) What Twins rookie pitcher toiled for 265-⅔ innings in 1978?

38) In 1977, when he earned the A.L. Most Valuable Player Award, Rod Carew led the league in which categories?

39) Slowed by injuries, Harmon Killebrew played in only 69 games in 1973 and had just 248 at-bats? How many homers did he hit?

40) Future Twins manager Tom Kelly played in 49 games with the team in 1975 and had 11 RBI in 127 at-bats. He hit his one and only homer that year in what park?

41) What Twins outfielder, know for his personable manner, led the A.L. in RBI's with 119 in 1977?

42) In 1979, who became the first Twins shortstop to start at that position in the All-Star game since Zoilo Versalles?

43) In the American League championship series in 1970, who stomped the Twins in three straight games, outscoring them 27-10?

44) When Rod Carew won the league batting title in 1972 at .318, what hitting oddity came along with it?

45) In what season of the decade of the 70's were the Twins in contention but finished fourth in the A.L. Western Division, 17.5 games behind champion Kansas City after losing 18 of its final 27 games?

46) On Aug. 10, 1971, Harmon Killebrew hit both his 500th and 501st career home runs at Met Stadium against what All-Star lefthander?

47) What Twins reliever had a 10-1 record in 1970 and a 1.99 ERA?

48) Who holds the Twins record for most shutouts in a season?

49) What Twins player nearly scored the 1,000,000th run in major-league on May 4, 1975 but was thrown out at the plate trying score from third on a sacrifice fly?

50) On April 25, 1977, two Twins pitchers were involved in an auto accident near Met Stadium and suffered serious injury. Who were they?

51) Who holds the Twins mark with most seasons played with 15?

52) Harmon Killebrew left the Twins after the '74 season and signed with Kansas City. On May 4, 1975, he returned with the Royals and had his number (3) retired in a pre-game ceremony. What happened in his first at-bat?

53) How many hits did Rod Carew amass while hitting .388 in 1977, the most in the majors since Bill Terry had 254 in 1930?

54) What Twins pitcher hit a homer in his second at-bat in his first game on September 7, 1970?

55) What position did the following players play for the Twins in the 1970's: Luis Gomez, Jose Ferrer, and Danny Thompson?

56) What Twins pitcher set the all-time major-league mark that still holds by finishing 84 games in 1979?

57) What Twins outfielder hit for the cycle on June 4, 1976?

58) What Twins catcher spent part of a season leading off for manager Gene Mauch, a big proponent of on-base percentage?

59) What Minnesota native started consecutive opening-day games on the mound from 1977-79?

60) What Twins first-baseman from the 1970's had a son playing for the team's AA club in New Britain, Connecticut in 2009?

1) New York Giants / San Francisco Giants (1956-60); Los Angeles Angels / California Angels (1961-69). The Angels were renamed in 1965 and today are known as the Los Angeles Angels of Anaheim.

2) 1971

3) Jim Perry. Incidentally, teammate Jim Kaat won his 179th later that year.

4) Hit the first home-run as a designated hitter. Oliva's first-inning homer off Catfish Hunter was on opening day, April 6th. (Ron Blomberg of the Yankees had come to bat as the first designated hitter earlier that day.)

5) Eddie Bane. The little lefty pitched well, allowing one run in seven innings but Kansas City eventually won 5-4. Bane went 0-5 in '73 and was 7-13 in parts of three seasons for the Twins.

6) Ty Cobb. Carew led the A.L. in 1972 (.318), 1973 (.350), 1974 (.364) and 1975 (.359).

7) George Brett (.333) and Hal McRae (.332).

8) Gary Serum. He pitched just eight innings in '77 but went 9-9 in 1978 in 23 starts before finishing his career in 1979 with a 1-3 mark.

9) Tom Johnson. His ERA was an impressive 3.12 in 71 games.

10) Bill "Soup" Campbell

11) Jim Shellenback. The 33-year-old lefthander pitched just 5 ⅔ innings in five appearances, ending a nine-year career with an overall record of 16-30 and an ERA of 3.81 in 165 games.

12) Bert Blyleven. Bert finished 20-17 with a 2.52 ERA and 258 strikeouts.

13) 81; Dan Ford led with 20 dingers and Larry Hisle added 14.

14) Jesse Orosco. The crafty lefty finished his career with 1,252 appearances in 24 seasons, posting an 87-80 record, 144 saves and an ERA of 3.16. Orosco pitched for nine teams from 1979 to 2003. He was 46 when he ended his career with the team who originally drafted him.

15) 1974. Harmon had just 13 homers and 54 RBI in 333 at-bats.

16) Butch Wynegar. In the ad, the narrator stated that Butch loved the game of baseball so much, he would play for nothing.

17) Mike Marshall

18) Rod Carew.

19) Eight. Carew was 239 for 616; 247 hits would have pushed him above .400.

20) April 6

21) Gene Mauch

22) .349. Oliva was 30-86 as a pinch-hitter, mostly from 1973-76.

23) Bobby Darwin

24) Dave Goltz. From 1974-76, the Rothsay, Minnesota native was 10-10, 14-14, and then 14-14. He was also 3-3 in 1972.

25) Larry Hisle. Larry clubbed 87 homers in five stellar seasons (1972-77).

26) Mike Marshall

27) John Castino. A spectacular fielder, Castino's career ended prematurely on account of a back injury early in '84. He hit .285 his rookie season.

28) Jerry Koosman. The lefty had went just 3-15 with the New York Mets in '78 and was 8-20 the year before that. "Koos" went 16-13 in '80.

29) Jose M. Morales

30) Washington Senators. Blyleven gave up a leadoff homer to Lee Maye.

31) Butch Wynegar. Possessing excellent fundamentals, Wynegar was a defensive stalwart and had a good stroke to go with a good eye.

32) Bobby Darwin

33) .334; Carew finished with a .328 lifetime average and 3,053 hits after completing his final seven seasons with California.

34) Steve Braun (left-handed hitter) and Steve Brye (right-handed hitter)

35) Jim Perry (24 – 1970); Bert Blyleven (20 – 1973); Dave Goltz (20 – 1977); and Jerry Koosman (20 – 1979)

36) Larry Hisle (Milwaukee) and Lyman Bostock (California)

37) Roger Erickson. The slender righthander went 14-13 with a 3.96 ERA but his promising career dwindled as he won just 13 games the next three seasons.

38) Hits (239), batting average (.388), runs scored (128), triples (16), intentional walks (15).

39) Five

40) Tiger Stadium against Vern Ruhle. Kelly was a lefty first-baseman.

41) Larry Hisle

42) Roy Smalley

43) Baltimore. The Orioles won 10-6, 11-3, and 6-1 to sweep the series.

44) Carew hit zero (0) homers.

45) 1977. Despite one of the top offenses in the league, the Twins were beset with pitching woes.

46) Mike Cuellar of the Baltimore Orioles.

47) Stan Williams, who had been traded from Cleveland with Luis Tiant in a blockbuster for Dean Chance, Graig Nettles, Bob Miller, and Ted Uhlaender.

48) Bert Blyleven had nine in 1973, leading the A.L.

49) Rod Carew. The Twins first-baseman was thrown out at home plate shortly before Houston Astro Bob Watson scored the momentous run at Candlestick Park in San Francisco. Watson, on second-base, scored on Milt May's three-run homer. He beat Cincinnati's Dave Concepcion by just 1.5 seconds to record that historic run.

50) Don Carrithers and Mike Pazik. Carrithers returned in July while Pazik missed the entire season. Carrithers pitched in only seven games in '77 and was 0-1 in 14-⅓ innings in his only season for the team. Pazik started three games and was 1-0 in 18 innings with a 2.50 earned-run-average but never pitched in the majors again.

51) Tony Oliva. Tony-O played from 1962-1976.

52) Killebrew homered to left. Harmon hit the three-run homer off Twins lefty Vic Albury. Later that season, he hit his final and 573rd homer of his illustrious career at the Bloomington ballpark off Minnesota lefthander Eddie Bane.

53) 239; Carew had 14 homers, 16 triples, 38 doubles, and 171 singles.

54) Hal Haydel. The righthander only took four more at-bats in his career but finished with a .500 batting average (3-6). Haydel hit the homer off of Milwaukee lefty A.L. Downing, who also served up Hank Aaron's record-breaking 715th home run in 1974.

55) Shortstop. Gomez played from 1974-77, Ferrer from 1974-75 and Thompson from 1970-76.

56) Mike Marshall. He also is tied for the all-time A.L. mark with 89 relief appearances in '79.

57) Larry Hisle. It took 10 innings and five at-bats but Hisle became the third man in team history to accomplish the feat at Baltimore. Later, on July 24, teammate Lyman Bostock also hit for the cycle at Chicago.

58) Butch Wynegar. In 1977, Wynegar often led off with his penchant for drawing walks. Rod Carew had relinquished his lead-off spot to bat third on his way to the M.V.P. award.

59) Dave Goltz. Born in Pelican Rapids, Goltz went on to win 49 games over those three seasons, including a 20-win season in '77.

60) Joe Lis. The elder Lis was the starter in '73 and hit .245 with nine homers. His son, Erik, has played five seasons of minor-league ball with the Twins.

Tom Brunansky

4

THE 1980s

1) Who was the last Twin to hit a homerun at Met Stadium?

2) How many times did Kent Hrbek either hit at least 30 homeruns or knock in at least 100 runs in a season?

3) What was the opening day line-up for the Twins in their first game at the Metrodome?

4) What Twins lefthander gave up Rod Carew's 3,000th hit at Anaheim Stadium on August 4, 1985?

5) In what two consecutive years did the Twins have the lowest attendance in the major leagues?

6) In what season did the Twins have 15 rookies on the roster for the majority of the season?

7) On July 31, 1984 Calvin Griffith sold 52% of the team to Carl Pohlad. What was the price?

8) In 1980, what player led the team in homers with just 13 and led the club in RBI with only 64, the two lowest totals in a full season in team history?

9) The 1986 Twins had five hitters who clubbed at least 20 homers for the first time since 1964? Who were they?

10) Whose 31-game hitting streak in 1980 was the longest in the A.L. since Boston's Dom DiMaggio hit in 34 straight in 1949?

11) In what year did a players' strike cause the major leagues to set up a first and second half and then a playoff to determine the overall winner?

12) What Twins reliever was released on June 6, 1980, and later claimed it was because of his "union activities"? (His formal grievance against the club wasn't upheld.)

13) In 1981, what three rookies homered in their first game in the majors for the Twins?

14) In what season did Kent Hrbek finish second in the MVP voting after hitting .311, slamming 27 homers, and knocking in 107 runs?

15) With seven games left in the regular season in 1984, the Twins were tied with Kansas City for the A.L. West lead. However, they lost the remainder of their games, including a game they lost 11-10 after building a 10-0 lead. What team beat them that night?

16) Kirby Puckett was the A.L. batting champion in 1989 with a .339 average. How many times did he finish second or third in the batting race?

17) Always noted for strong defense under the tutelage of manager Tom Kelly, the Twins set a then major-league record for the least errors in 1988. How many did they commit?

18) What rookie reliever had a sensational year in 1980 with an 8-6 record, an ERA of 1.99, and 23 saves?

19) Who managed the Twins after Gene Mauch resigned on August 24, 1980, and was re-signed the next year after the team finished 23-13?

20) When the Twins moved from Metropolitan Stadium to the Metrodome after the 1981 season, how many miles did they move?

21) On September 30, 1981—a chilly, rainy, day—the Twins played their final game at Metropolitan Stadium, losing 5-2 to what division foe?

22) Can you name the two Yankees (a reliever and a shortstop) the Twins received in early 1982 as part of the deal that sent Roy Smalley to New York?

23) What two Twins were traded to California early in the '82 season in exchange for Tom Brunansky and pitcher Mike Walters?

24) Despite some terrific offensive numbers (.301 average, 23 HR, 92 RBI), a 23-game hitting streak and an All-Star selection, first-baseman Kent Hrbek finished second in the 1982 Rookie-of-the-Year voting to what A.L. player?

25) What two regulars hit over .300 for the 1983 Twins squad?

26) What off-season acquisition led the Twins in pitching wins with 13 in 1982?

27) In what year did the Twins become the first A.L. team to attract more than 3 million fans in a season?

28) What reliever (closer) led the team in saves for four straight seasons in the 1980's but was booed unmercifully when he struggled?

29) What Twins slugger hit 31 round-trippers in his third season after hitting just four homers total in his first two seasons?

30) Who became the second Twins hurler to win the Cy Young award after going 24-7 in 1988?

31) What Twins lefty, called up from AAA Portland early in the '88 season, went on to lead the A.L. in ERA with a 2.45 mark along with a 16-9 log?

32) Prior to the 1989 season, the Twins lost closer Jeff Reardon to what A.L. team to a huge, 3-year, $14 million contract?

33) What native Minnesotan was the first Twins batter to hit in the Metrodome on April 6, 1982?

34) What Twins infielder, who played for the club from 1982-86 as a reserve, was the last man cut on the '87 club, thus missing a chance to win a World Series ring?

35) What Hall of Fame pitcher won 329 games in his career but just one with the Twins?

36) Believe it or not, the lowest RBI total to lead the club for a single season is 37 in the shortened season of 1981 (109 games). Who was the player?

37) Who hit the first inside-the-park grand slam homer in Twins history on July 19, 1982 in the Metrodome?

38) Kirby Puckett holds the team single-game mark for most total bases with how many?

39) What lone Twins representative in the All-Star game at the Metrodome in 1985 had the pivotal homer to help the A.L. win the first home-run derby? (He finished second in the individual contest with four homers but went 0-1 in the actual game.)

40) What catcher holds the Twins single-game record for throwing out four runners against the Yankees on May 29, 1982?

41) When Bert Blyleven set the major-league mark for home runs allowed in a season in 1986, how many did he give up?

42) What position did the following Twins players play in the 1980's: Glenn Adams, Danny Goodwin, and Gene Larkin?

43) What Twins player became the first elected to the Hall of Fame on January 10, 1984, in his fourth year of eligibility?

44) What Twins batter had a 17-game and a 23-game hitting streak in his rookie season?

45) What event with enormous portent for the Twins took place on April 19, 1983?

46) What Twins pitcher of Panamanian extraction went 33-13 in four impressive seasons as a middle reliever (1987-90)?

47) In 1984, this left-handed hitter hit a homer off Jack Morris in his first at-bat and never hit another in 37 more career games?

48) What Twins player hit two inside-the-park homers in the penultimate game of 1986?

49) In what year did the Twins have a streak of 26 straight games with attendance in excess of 30,000 per game?

50) Which Twins outfielder tied a major-league record with three triples in a game against Texas on July 3, 1980?

51) What Twins player holds the team record for the highest seasonal fielding percentage for an outfielder at .997?

52) The shortest and longest nine-inning games in Twins history came against the same opponent in the 1980's? Who was it?

53) For four straight seasons, what two Twins fielders won Gold Gloves at their positions?

54) Who was the first Twins pitcher to pinch-hit since the advent of the DH in 1973?

55) What two starting right-handed pitchers did the Twins receive from Texas in exchange for outfielder Gary Ward prior to the '84 season?

56) What two remarkable individual accomplishments took place in a game between the Twins and Oakland on August 1, 1986?

57) Who were the five managers who guided the Twins during the 1980's?

58) What valuable infield reserve was acquired from Montreal prior to the 1987 season and played a pivotal defensive role for two world champions?

59) Did Kent Hrbek play a full season at Met Stadium in his hometown of Bloomington ?

60) What Twin Cities' product was the primary catcher for the team in the 1980's, hitting for a paltry average but reaching double-digits in homers four times?

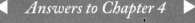

1) Pete Mackanin, a reserve infielder, hit it on the last day of the season.

2) Hrbek hit 30 homers once (34 in 1987) and knocked in 100 runs once (107 in 1984).

3) Jim Eisenreich CF
   Gary Ward DH
   Dave Engle RF
   Roy Smalley SS
   Kent Hrbek 1B
   Gary Gaetti 3B
   Butch Wynegar C
   Rob Wilfong 2B
   Mickey Hatcher LF
   Pete Redfern P

4) Frank Viola. Carew's milestone hit was typical, a liner to left field.

5) 1980 (769,206) and 1981 (469,090)

6) 1982. While that team went 60-102, youngsters like Hrbek, Gaetti, Viola, and Brunansky got the experience that would prove invaluable.

7) $34 million

8) John Castino. The Chicago-area native also hit .302 for this anemic offense.

9) Gary Gaetti (34), Kirby Puckett (31), Kent Hrbek (29), Tom Brunansky (23) and Roy Smalley (20).

10) Ken Landreaux

11) 1981. The Twins went 17-39 in the first half and 24-29 in the second half.

12) Mike Marshall

13) Kent Hrbek, Gary Gaetti, and Tim Laudner. Interestingly, they combined for only nine total homers, as they were all late-season call-ups.

14) 1984. Detroit reliever Willie Hernandez was the MVP.

15) Cleveland

16) Puckett finished 2nd twice (1988 and 1992) and third once (1986).

17) 84 (the previous mark was 91)

18) Doug Corbett. He went on to make the '81 A.L. All-Star team.

19) Johnny Goryl. Unfortunately, he was dismissed early in '81 after his team struggled to a 11-25 start and Billy Gardner took over the manager role.

20) The distance is 8.8 miles.

21) Kansas City Royals. The attendance at the final game was 15,900. Coincidentally, the Vikings' closed out their final season in December of 1981 with a 10-6 loss to another Kansas City team, the NFL Chiefs.

22) Ron Davis (reliever) and Greg Gagne (shortstop)

23) Doug Corbett (reliever) and Rob Wilfong (second baseman)

24) Cal Ripken (Baltimore shortstop)

25) Mickey Hatcher (.317) and Dave Engle (.305)

26) Bobby Castillo

27) In 1988, when they drew 3,030,672; the Los Angeles Dodgers were the first team to attract three million.

28) Ron Davis

29) Kirby Puckett (1986)

30) Frank Viola. "Sweet Music" was outstanding, compiling a 2.64 ERA.

31) Allan Anderson

32) Boston Red Sox

33) Jim Eisenreich. Unfortunately, the former St. Cloud Tech star could not overcome the affects of Tourette Syndrome and the centerfielder played in just 34 games, hitting .303. He played just two games in '83 and 12 in '84 before retiring. In one of baseball's best stories, Jim made a comeback with the Kansas City Royals in 1987 and went on to play in the World Series with the Phillies later in his career.

34) Ron Washington, who is presently the manager of the Texas Rangers.

35) Steve Carlton. "Lefty" went 1-6 in his brief stint in Minnesota in nine games at the end of the '87 season and four contests early in the '88 season before his release and eventual retirement. Carlton had won at least 10 games for 18 straight seasons with St. Louis and Philadelphia from 1967-1984.

36) Mickey Hatcher

37) Tom Brunansky

38) 14. Puckett's magical day in Milwaukee on August 30, 1987 consisted of two homers, two doubles, and two singles. He had gone 4-5 the previous day and his 10 hits in two-consecutive games tied a major-league record.

39) Tom Brunansky

40) Sal Butera

41) 50; the next year Blyleven allowed 46.

42) Designated Hitter and/or First Base

43) Harmon Killebrew. "Harm" received 83% of the vote total and was joined in the Hall of Fame by shortstop Luis Aparicio and pitcher Don Drysdale.

44) Kent Hrbek. The Bloomington native hit .301 overall in 1982 with 23 homers and 92 RBI.

45) Joseph Patrick Mauer is born in St. Paul to parents Teresa and Jake Mauer.

46) Juan Berenguer

47) Andre David. The left-handed hitter became the eighth Twins hitter to hit a homer in his first-ever game, at Tiger Stadium on June 29, and the fourth to do so in his first at-bat.

48) Greg Gagne

49) 1988. The streak went from June 22 to August 24 and included seven crowds of over 40,000, and four over 50,000 from July 8-22.

50) Ken Landreaux

51) Bobby Mitchell. In 1982, Mitchell made one error and had 350 putouts.

52) Toronto. On Sept. 28, 1982, the Twins and Jays' played a game in a rapid 1 hour 33 minutes. On July 25, 1987, the same clubs labored to finish in 4 hours and five minutes.

53) Gary Gaetti (third base) and Kirby Puckett (outfield) from 1986-89.

54) Allan Anderson (struck out)

55) John Butcher and Mike Smithson

56) Bert Blyleven notched his 3,000 strikeout while tying a team record with 15 strikeouts and Kirby Puckett hit for the cycle.

57) Gene Mauch (1980), Johnny Goryl (1980-81), Billy Gardner (1981-85), Ray Miller (1985-86), Tom Kelly (1986-89). Kelly managed through 2001.

58) Al Newman. Handling a tiny glove, Newman was a tremendous backup at second-base, shortstop, and third-base.

59) No. Hrbek was called up in late August of 1981 and he played in just 24 games that season and batted .239 in 67 at-bats.

60) Tim Laudner (Brooklyn Park). Laudner hit just .225 in his 734-game career, all with the Twins. Tim, however, batted .318 in the '87 World Series.

Paul Molitor

5

THE 1990s

1) Kirby Puckett hit a grand slam on August 10, 1994, in the Twins' final game of that strike-shortened season. What Twins player played his last game on that day?

2) Kirby Puckett totaled 2,040 hits in his first 10 years in the big leagues, a feat exceeded by only one other player. Who was he?

3) What Twins catcher posted the longest hitting streak in the majors in 1990?

4) What two Twins righthanders set a club record with 12 straight wins while hurling for Minnesota in the 1990's?

5) When the Twins executed their two triple plays against Boston on July 17, 1990, did they win or lose?

6) In 1992 what trio of Twins became the first in club history to score 100 runs each in a season?

7) In 1993 who became just the second Twins hitter (Harmon Killebrew was the first) to reach the career milestone of 1,000 RBIs?

8) What Twins hitter had no grand slam homers in his first six seasons but then slugged three during the 1992 season?

9) What Twins catcher became just the fourth catcher in 40 years to hit .300 or higher three consecutive seasons?

10) When St. Paul native Dave Winfield collected his 3,000th hit as a Twin on Sept. 16, 1993, at the Metrodome, what Hall of Fame pitcher gave up his ninth-inning single?

11) In the first year after the major leagues were realigned from east-west divisions to an east-central-west scenario, the Twins landed in the A.L. Central with what other teams?

12) What Twins second baseman led the majors in doubles in 1994 with 45?

13) On Sept. 13, 1993, Terry Ryan became the Twins general manager. Who did he replace? (Hint: the man left to become president of the Chicago Cubs.)

14) The 1995 season started late due to a strike. Who won the A.L. Central that year?

15) Despite a shorter schedule of 144 games in 1995, the Twins finished more games out of first place that in any other season? How far behind were they at season's end?

16) What Twins player recorded his 1,000th run and his 1,000th RBI within 10 days of each other in May 1995?

17) Who did the Twins receive in a trade for Dave Hollins in September 1996?

18) Who became the Twins fifth player to be named A.L. Rookie-of-the-Year in 1995 after hitting .277 with 24 homers, 84 RBI, and 20 stolen bases?

19) In his last plate appearance in the major-leagues, Kirby Puckett was struck in the face on Sept. 28, 1995 by what Cleveland righthander?

20) Prior to the 1997 season, what native-Minnesota catcher, who had won a World Series with his previous team, signed a free-agent contract with the Twins?

21) Interleague play started in 1997. Who was the first N.L. team the Twins played that year?

22) On Feb. 6, 1998, the Twins traded All-Star Chuck Knoblauch to the New York Yankees for what four players?

23) In 1996, what Twins hitter led the A.L. in hits, was second in at-bats, and tied for third in batting average (.341)?

24) What player did the Twins acquire in the Rule 5 draft from San Diego prior to the 1990 season who went on to hit .326 as an outfielder?

25) What pitcher became the fourth Twins hurler to pitch a no-hitter on September 11, 1999, versus the Anaheim Angels?

26) What actual eye disorder caused Kirby Puckett to suffer from blurred vision on March 28, 1996, leading to his eventual retirement on July 12?

27) What Twins pitcher led the majors in losses with 19 in 1993?

28) In a year when the Twins played 17 rookies in 1999, which one playing at first-base led the majors in fielding percentage at .997?

29) On April 27, 1994, what Twins righthander pitched a no-hitter at the Metrodome against the Milwaukee Brewers?

30) In what year did the Twins set all-time club highs that still stand for team batting average (.288), runs scored (877), hits (1,663), and RBI (812)?

31) On July 17, 1990, the Twins turned two triple plays against Boston at Fenway Park. Amazingly, the same three players combined to execute both of them in the exact same fashion. Who were the fielders?

32) What member of the 1991 World Champion Twins club hit .303 in part-time duty at first-base and the outfield?

33) What position did the following players play in the 1990's: Matt Walbeck, Derek Parks, and Greg Myers?

34) What left-handed reliever got so much better with experience that he was voted the "Most Improved" Twins player in both 1990 and 1992?

35) What future Twins player hit for the cycle and went 5-5 batting against Minnesota's Kevin Tapani on May 15, 1991?

36) What Twins starter has made the most Opening Day starts?

37) What Twins player played in only 108 games in the strike-shortened 1994 season but led the A.L. with 112 runs-batted-in?

38) What Twins righthander, acquired in the Viola trade in 1989, led the team in wins four times in the 1990's?

39) On Oct. 2, 1992, what batter joined Roy Smalley as the only Twins to hit homers from both sides of the plate in the same game?

40) What pinch-hitter set the club record with 19 pinch-hits during the 1996 season?

41) What Twins catcher hit .335 in backup duty in 1990 (71 games) and wore number "O"?

42) What former Yankee platooned with Scott Leius at third base in 1991 after Gary Gaetti had served nine years as the starter?

43) Since 1997, when the program was initiated, the Twins have one of the best inter-league records in baseball; what is their won-loss log?

44) What two great milestones did Cal Ripken reach at the Metrodome?

45) The Twins unveiled a large curtain in the upper deck above right-field in the same year they open a plaza along the west side of the Metrodome called Kirby Puckett Place? What year was it?

46) What Twins runner was the last to have a "pure" steal of home?

47) What Twins lefthander tied for the A.L. lead with three shutouts in 1996 yet had an unimpressive ERA of 5.12 and a lackluster 7-17 record?

48) What team broke the Minnesota Twins longest winning streak ever when Randy Milligan knocked in the game-winning run at Memorial Stadium on June 17, 1991?

49) What Twins outfield duo, who manned most of the games in right and left field in '99, were also teammates on the 1996 U.S. Olympic baseball team?

50) What two Twins finished tied for third in the A.L. batting race in 1996 behind Alex Rodriguez (.358) and Frank Thomas (.349)?

51) What former Louisiana State All-American and top draft choice in '94 led the Twins in hitting in 1998 at .316?

52) What position did the following Twins play for the club in the 1990's: Dan Masteller, Steve Dunn, David McCarty, and Greg Colbrunn?

53) What Twins relief pitcher, who has the highest total of appearances in club history, started 16 games in 1993 before finding his niche in the bullpen?

54) On July 5, 1992, what Twins designated-hitter lost a sure home-run when his towering drive to right hit a speaker and caromed into the glove of Oriole second baseman Mark McLemore for an out?

55) The longest game in Twins history (time, not innings) occurred on May 7, 1995, when visiting Minnesota won 10-9 in 17 innings against which A.L. foe?

56) On Aug. 31, 1993, the Twins tied their all-time mark for most innings played when they beat Cleveland 5-4 at the Metrodome. How many innings did they play?

57) Who is the only position player to pitch in more than one game in a season for Minnesota?

58) Who is the only Twins player to play 100 games or more at shortstop, second-base, third-base, and the outfield?

59) Righthander Scott Erickson pitched the only complete-game one-hitter for the Twins in the 1990's. Which Red Sox batter got the only hit that day (July 24, 1992)?

60) When Yankee lefthander David Wells completed his perfect game against the Twins on May 17, 1998, who was the last batter to be retired?

1) Kent Hrbek. The author was lucky enough to catch Puckett's drive into the third row of the left-center-field bleachers, albeit with eyes closed.

2) "Wee" Willie Keeler (2,065). Incredibly, Ichiro Suzuki has 2,030 in just nine seasons (2001-09) with the Seattle Mariners.

3) Brian Harper (25)

4) Scott Erickson (1991) and Brad Radke (1997)

5) Boston won 1-0 with Tom Bolton besting Scott Erickson.

6) Chuck Knoblauch, Shane Mack, and Kirby Puckett (1992)

7) Kent Hrbek. "Herbie" finished with 1,086 RBI, one ahead of Kirby Puckett (1,085) but well behind Harmon Killebrew's total of 1,325.

8) Kirby Puckett

9) Brian Harper. Harper hit .311 in 1991, .307 in '92, and .304 in '93.

10) Dennis Eckersley

11) Chicago White Sox, Cleveland Indians, Kansas City Royals, and Milwaukee Brewers. In 1994, three teams from the former A.L. West (Chicago, Kansas City, and Minnesota) joined together with two teams from the former A.L. East (Cleveland and Milwaukee) to form the new five-team division. When the N.L. expanded in 1998, Milwaukee switched to the National League and began playing in the N.L. Central while Detroit switched from the A.L. East to the A.L. Central.

12) Chuck Knoblauch

13) Andy MacPhail

14) Cleveland Indians. It was the first title of any kind for the Indians since winning the A.L. pennant in 1954.

15) 44 games. Minnesota had a 56-88 record.

16) Kirby Puckett

17) David Ortiz. From 1997-2002, Ortiz showed power potential but was injury-prone and erratic. David became one of the game's top

sluggers after signing as a free agent with Boston and helping end Boston's World Series drought in 2004.

18) Marty Cordova. Other Twins to win the award were Tony Oliva (1964), Rod Carew (1967), John Castino (1979), and Chuck Knoblauch (1991).

19) Dennis Martinez. The blow broke Puckett's jaw.

20) Terry Steinbach, the Oakland star from New Ulm.

21) Houston Astros

22) Pitcher Eric Milton, outfielder Brian Buchanan, shortstop Cristian Guzman, and pitcher Daniel Mota.

23) Paul Molitor. At age 40, Molitor had 225 hits, 660 at-bats and 113 RBIs.

24) Shane Mack

25) Eric Milton

26) Glaucoma

27) Scott Erickson. The righthander was just 8-19 with a 5.19 ERA just two seasons removed from going 20-8 with a 3.18 ERA.

28) Doug Mientkiewicz

29) Scott Erickson

30) 1996; incidentally, all this was done without Kirby Puckett, who was forced to retire after suffering eye damage during spring training.

31) 3B Gary Gaetti, 2B A.L. Newman, 1B Kent Hrbek.

32) Randy Bush

33) Catcher

34) Mark Guthrie

35) Paul Molitor, who was playing for the Milwaukee Brewers.

36) Brad Radke (8). Bert Blyleven has started six and Frank Viola four.

37) Kirby Puckett. Averaging an RBI per game, how fun would it have been to see how many runs Kirby could have knocked in for a full season?

38) Kevin Tapani. The Escanaba, Michigan native led in wins in '90, '93, and '94, and tied with John Smiley in 1992.

39) Chili Davis. Smalley connected from both sides on May 30, 1986.

40) Chip Hale

41) Junior Ortiz

42) Mike Pagliarulo.

43) 132 wins and 97 losses (1997-2009)

44) Ripken played in his 2,000th consecutive game on his way to his astounding record of 2,632 consecutive games played and he also collected his 3,000th hit on April 15, 2000, against Hector Carrasco. When Ripken reached first-base, he was congratulated by Oriole first-base coach, Eddie Murray, his former teammate, who also got his 3,000th hit in Minneapolis.

45) 1996

46) Rich Becker. The centerfielder stole home on Sept. 27, 1997 against Cleveland, just the 11th "pure" steal of home in Twins history.

47) Rich Robertson. He tied for the league lead in shutouts with Ken Hill of Texas and Pat Hentgen of Toronto.

48) Baltimore Orioles. The moment was immortalized in the classic movie *A Few Good Men*, at least if you are paying attention. Milligan's double scored both the tying and game-winning runs.

49) Chad Allen and Jacque Jones

50) Chuck Knoblauch and Paul Molitor, who both ended the season at .341.

51) Todd Walker.

52) First Base

53) Eddie Guardado, who pitched in 648 games. Rick Aguilera had 490.

54) Chili Davis

55) Cleveland Indians. The marathon contest lasted 6 hours and 36 minutes.

56) 22. Brett Merriman was the winning pitcher in a game that took 6:17. The other 22-inning saga took place on May 12, 1972, at Metropolitan Stadium when the Milwaukee Brewers finally won 4-3 in 5:47 as Jim Colborn bested Bert Blyleven. It was suspended after 21 innings and completed the next day.

57) John Moses. In 1990, the outfielder pitched in two road games. He pitched an inning at Boston on May 19 and gave up a run and he also pitched an inning at California on July 31 and gave up two runs. In 1989, Moses also hurled an inning at Boston, allowing just a walk with no hits.

58) Denny Hocking. The versatile reserve played 277 games at shortstop, 267 at second-base, 118 at third-base, and 211 in the outfield (93 in right, 50 in center, and 58 in left). He even played 43 games at first-base.

59) Tom Brunansky. The former Twins rightfielder had grounded into a triple play against Erickson on July 17, 1990, at Fenway, an interesting twist.

60) Shortstop Pat Meares, who flied out to right-fielder Paul O'Neill to end the 4-0 loss.

Brad Radke

6

THE 2000s

1) Who is the only Twins pitcher to get a hit in the Metrodome?

2) What number uniform was worn by Twins standout lefthander Johan Santana from 2000 to 2007?

3) What Kansas City player walked in the top of the 9th inning to ruin Scott Baker's perfect game bid on August 31, 2007, at the Metrodome; and who later singled to ruin his no-hit bid?

4) What Twins infielder won a Gold Glove in 2001 and also hit .306?

5) What threesome made up the so-called Soul Patrol outfield for the Twins in the early 2000's?

6) Who broke Bert Blyleven's 1973 club record of 258 single-season strikeouts?

7) In what years has Twins catcher Joe Mauer won A.L. batting titles?

8) In what year did the Minnesota Twins earn the "Organization of the Year" award by Baseball America?

9) What Twins rookie startled the baseball world with his superlative performance on the mound in 2006?

10) Tom Kelly managed in 2,385 games as the Twins manager. How many games was he ejected from?

11) What Twins outfielder led the team in hitting at .305 in 2000 and earned a berth on the A.L. All-Star squad?

12) In 2006, what Park Center High graduate arrived on the scene as a rookie reliever and became a sensation as an eighth-inning set-up man before elbow injuries cost him most of the 2008 season and all of 2009?

13) Joe Mauer made his major-league debut in April of 2004 but his highly-anticipated arrival was cut short by an injury that limited him to just 35 games that season. What was the injury?

14) Who is the only Twins pitcher to win the Triple Crown (wins, ERA, and strikeouts)?

15) The Twins became the first team to win a division or pennant after trailing by three games with four games left in 2009? What team did they tie and then defeat in a one-game playoff at the Metrodome?

16) On the night that the 35W bridge over the Mississippi River collapsed a few blocks from the Metrodome in August of 2007, who were the Twins playing?

17) Which Twins reliever set a then Twins record with 45 saves while leading the American League in 2002?

18) Who is the only Twins pitcher to record six straight seasons with at least 35 saves?

19) What two former Twins teammates were inducted into the Baseball Hall of Fame together on Aug. 5, 2001?

20) Who set the team single-game strikeout mark with 17 in an August 19, 2007, home game against the Texas Rangers?

21) During the early years of the 2000's, the Twins sported an international infield. Who did it consist of?

22) What is the Twins record for most consecutive losing seasons?

23) The Twin started the 2008 season with four starters age 26 or younger; all had double-digit victory seasons. Who were they?

24) When Justin Morneau hit 34 homers in 2006, he became the first Twin to hit at least 30 in a season since three players did so in 1987? Who were they?

25) How many days were the Twins in first place when they won the A.L. Central in 2006?

26) What Twins pitcher led the team in 2001 with 17 wins, an ERA of 3.16, and 233-⅔ innings, and then, after signing a long-term contract, garnered only 18 more victories in a Twins uniform?

27) In 2002, Torii Hunter (29) and Jacque Jones (27) led the Twins in homers, but who was the DH who was third with 20?

28) What former #1 draft pick was called up from the minors in 2001 and went 1-2 with an ERA of 8.28 that season and would pitch just 1-⅓ more innings (2003) for the team before being released?

29) What Rochester Mayo graduate with power potential hit just three home runs for the Twins in 113 at-bats over parts of three seasons (2002-2004)?

30) Durable Torii Hunter had his season cut short in 2005 when he fractured his ankle attempting to make a catch on July 29 at Fenway Park. Despite playing in just 98 games, did he earn a Gold Glove?

31) Who is the only one of Joe Mauer's teammates to have exceeded him in on-base percentage among regulars during a season?

32) What Twins second baseman set the major-league mark for errorless games at that position in 2007 only to have Detroit's Placido Polanco break it a few months later?

33) What Twins player led the majors in bunt singles in 2008 (30), breaking Rod Carew's single-season mark?

34) What Twins reliever blew nine of 37 save opportunities in 2001, leading to the ascent of Eddie Guardado as the closer in 2002?

35) What Twins player stole 12 bases in 2002 but was caught stealing 13 times?

36) What Twins utility player has been perhaps the team's most versatile defensively since Cesar Tovar?

37) What Twins infielder set a club record for stolen-base percentage when he was successful in 15 of 16 attempts in 2004 (15 attempts minimum)?

38) What major post-season awards did the Twins win in 2006?

39) What Twins call-up in 2005, a third-baseman, hit .425 (17 for 40) in 13 games that year but never played another game in the Major Leagues?

40) What Twins pitcher gave up less than 6 hits per start in 2005 yet won only 16 games?

41) What Twins rookie hurler led the team in games started (33) in 2008 and also started the one-game playoff game in Chicago that the White Sox won 1-0 to win the A.L. Central title?

42) What Twins reliever went 0-7 in 2000 despite having a solid 3.65 ERA and giving up less than a hit per inning?

43) A great two-strike hitter, this impressive young batter was traded away after the 2003 season despite recording a .300 or higher batting average in three of his four previous seasons. Who was he?

44) In 2001, the Twins had two pitchers with at least 10 saves. Who were they?

45) Did Torii Hunter, the sensational center-fielder, ever hit 30 home runs for the Twins or knock in at least 100 runs in a season?

46) What Twins player was acquired at the All-Star break in 2003 from Toronto, and despite playing in only 65 games for the team, finished 4th in the A.L. MVP balloting that year?

47) What Twin played in 476 games and hit a respectable .261 in six seasons with the team, but never stole a base?

48) What two players, both former Yankees, split time as the designated hitters in 2006 and struggled?

49) Who replaced Luis Castillo after the second baseman was traded to the New York Mets in the midst of the 2007 season?

50) What is the hometown and province of Canadian third-baseman Corey Koskie, who played with distinction for the Twins from 1998 to 2004?

51) What three brothers all played in the Twins minor-league system in the early 2000's?

52) Who is the manager of the Ft. Myers Miracle minor-league team for the Twins in 2010 after leading the Gulf Coast Twins Rookie team to the League title in 2009?

53) What current Twins relief pitcher was born in Toronto, Canada?

54) Who is the only Twins hitter to hit at least 20 homers and steal at least 20 bases in a single season twice?

55) What Twins pitcher has the best ERA in Twins history (minimum 200 games) and also the lowest opponent batting average?

56) What pitcher has pitched relief in the most games in Twins history?

57) Catcher Mike Redmond, an extremely valuable backup to Joe Mauer from 2005 to 2009, had 1,415 total chances and 1,340 putouts during that period. How many errors did he make ?

58) What Twins pitcher, a Minnesota native, was also a second-team All-American at the University of Minnesota and was the 22nd overall selection in the 2004 amateur draft?

59) What is the largest deficit ever overcome in a Minnesota victory?

60) What former Twin has served as the infield/base-running coordinator for the minor-league system for most of the 2000's?

61) For the first time in their history in 2009, the Twins had four hitters knock in at least 90 runs in a season. Who were they?

62) Joe Mauer set a major-league mark for the highest batting average by a catcher in a single season (100 games minimum) in 2009. What was his final average?

63) What two Twins batters hit for the cycle in games played at the Metrodome in 2009?

64) What Twins left-handed starter in 2009 pitched for the 2008 U.S. Olympic team in Beijing?

65) The Twins played a total of 2,242 regular-season games at the Metrodome from 1982 to 2009. In which game did they set the all-time single-game attendance mark and what significance did the game have?

66) What Twins slugger set a team record by hitting two homers in a single inning on August 23, 2009?

67) What Twins hurler went 17 straight starts without a road loss during 2004 and 2005?

68) On March 22, 2010, Joe Mauer signed the fourth-largest contract in major league history with the Twins. For how many years and how much money did he sign?

69) What pitcher tied a major-league record with four wild pitches in a single inning against the Twins and joined the Minnesota staff the next year?

1) Bobby Korecky. The reliever had a single in an extra-inning win over Texas on May 19, 2008. He also won the game.

2) 57

3) John Buck walked and after an out, pinch-hitter Mike Sweeney followed with a single to center. Baker did earn his shutout (5-0).

4) Doug Mientkiewicz

5) Torii Hunter, Jacque Jones, and Matt Lawton

6) Johan Santana. He set the mark of 265 in 2004.

7) Mauer won in 2006 (.347), 2008 (.328), and 2009 (.365).

8) 2002

9) Francisco Liriano. He was 12-3 with a 2.16 ERA and 144 strikeouts in 121 innings and just 89 hits. A late-season elbow injury cost him the entire 2007 season.

10) Five. Kelly was noted for rarely getting upset or angry, at least on the field.

11) Matt Lawton

12) Pat Neshek

13) Knee injury. Joe injured himself sliding to catch a pop-up in just his second game.

14) Johan Santana. The Venezuelan had 19 wins, a 2.77 ERA, and 245 strikeouts in 2006. Santana won the A.L. Cy Young award.

15) Detroit. The Twins went 4-0 in their final four contests while the Tigers were 1-3 as both teams finished 86-76. On Oct. 6, in a one-game playoff, Minnesota won 6-5 in 12 innings to win the A.L. Central.

16) Kansas City. The Royals won 5-3 but the Twins postponed the afternoon game slated for the next day.

17) Eddie Guardado. Joe Nathan surpassed it with 47 saves in '09.

18) Joe Nathan. Here are Joe's totals since his arrival from San Francisco in the trade for A.J. Pierzynski: 2004 (44); 2005 (43); 2006 (36); 2007 (37); 2008 (39); 2009 (47).

19) Dave Winfield and Kirby Puckett, who played together in 1993 and 1994.

20) Johan Santana. He pitched only 8 innings to record the 17 Ks.

21) 1B- Doug Mientkiewicz (U.S.) 2B – Luis Rivas (Venezuela) SS – Cristian Guzman (Dominican Republic) 3B – Corey Koskie (Canada)

22) Eight. The Twins had losing seasons from 1993-2000.

23) Scott Baker, Nick Blackburn, Glen Perkins, and Kevin Slowey

24) Kent Hrbek (34), Gary Gaetti (31), and Tom Brunansky (32)

25) One day. The Twins defeated Chicago on the last day of the season at the Metrodome and then watched visiting Kansas City defeat Detroit which allowed them to win the division by one game.

26) Joe Mays

27) David Ortiz, who went on to greater fame after leaving the Twins.

28) Adam Johnson

29) Michael Restovich

30) Yes

31) Lew Ford. The outfielder (.381) outdid Mauer (.369) in 2004.

32) Luis Castillo

33) Carlos Gomez broke Carew's mark of 29, set in 1974.

34) LaTroy Hawkins

35) Cristian Guzman

36) Denny Hocking. This valuable player played 11 years for the Twins and once played 10 or more games at seven positions in 2000.

37) Luis Rivas

38) MVP (Justin Morneau); Cy Young (Johan Santana); Executive of the Year (Terry Ryan); Minor League Player of the Year (Matt Garza)

39) Glenn Williams

40) Johan Santana. Poor run support cost Santana the chance to win three straight Cy Young awards as Bartolo Colon won for the Angels.

41) Nick Blackburn

42) Bob Wells

43) A. J. Pierzynski. The young catcher was traded because Joe Mauer was the heir apparent. The Twins, of course, got Joe Nathan, Francisco Liriano, and Boof Bonser in return.

44) LaTroy Hawkins (28) and Eddie Guardado (12)

45) Yes. Hunter slugged 31 homers in '06 and knocked in 100 runs twice (102 in '03 and 107 in '07).

46) Shannon Stewart. Batting leadoff, Stewart's excellent at-bats and clutch hitting were an inspiration. He hit .322 and had an on-base percentage of .384. Bobby Kielty was dealt in exchange for Stewart.

47) Matthew LeCroy

48) Rondell White and Ruben Sierra

49) Alexi Casilla

50) Anola, Manitoba

51) Joe, Jake, and Bill Mauer. Jake was an infielder and Bill, a pitcher. Joe played three seasons in the minors, Jake five seasons as an infielder, and Bill three as a pitcher.

52) Jake Mauer. The 30-year-old older brother of Joe Mauer has shown promise as a manager and is hoping to manage in the big leagues some day.

53) Jesse Crain. Crain is 32-20 in five seasons with Minnesota.

54) Torii Hunter (2002 and 2004)

55) Joe Nathan. The lanky righthander has an eye-popping 1.87 ERA in 418-⅔ innings in 412 games and a .185 opponent batting average.

56) Eddie Guardado (623) while Rick Aguilera relieved in 460.

57) None. Redmond's errorless streak is an American League record.

58) Glen Perkins

59) Seven. On May 10, 2000, the Twins trailed Cleveland 8-1 before winning 10-9.

60) Paul Molitor, who is considered one of the best and smartest base-runners in major-league history.

61) Justin Morneau (100); Justin Kubel (103), Joe Mauer (96), and Michael Cuddyer (94).

62) .365 (Mauer holds a .327 lifetime mark following the 2009 season.)

63) Jason Kubel and Michael Cuddyer. Kubel's feat came on April 17 in a 11-9 victory over the Angels as he became just the seventh player in major-league history to hit a grand slam as part of the cycle. Cuddyer's cycle happened on May 22 in a 11-3 win over Milwaukee. Cuddyer's feat was completed when he tripled on a broken-bat grounder down the left-field line. Kubel and Cuddyer became the ninth and 10th Twins to hit for the cycle, joining Lyman Bostock and Larry Hisle (1976) as the only pair to do so in the same season.

64) Brian Duensing.

65) On Oct. 6, 2009, the paid attendance was 54,088 for the one-game playoff to determine the A.L. Central title. Beyond that, it was significant in that it was the last game played during the regular season at the Dome. (The previous record had been 53,106 when the Twins beat Kansas City on Sept. 27, 1987.)

66) Michael Cuddyer. The former first-round pick in 1997 hit two homers in the 7th inning of a 10-3 win over the Royals. He is the 53rd player in the majors to accomplish the feat. He is the only player to hit two home runs in an inning and also hit for the cycle in the same season in major-league history.

67) Johan Santana.

68) Eight years and $184 million.

69) R.A. Dickey, a right-handed knuckle-baller for the Mariners, tied the mark on Aug, 17, 2008, and joined the Twins relief corps in 2009.

7

KIDS STUFF

1) What is the name of the Twins mascot?

2) What are the Minnesota Twins named after?

3) What is the number of Twins catcher and hometown hero Joe Mauer?

4) What former Twins pitcher and TV broadcaster enjoys "circling" Twins fans on during telecasts?

5) In what inning do the fans rise and sing "Take Me Out To The Ballgame?

6) What team bats first when the Twins play at home?

7) In what city will the Twins be playing when Target Field opens in April of 2010?

8) From what side of the plate do both Joe Mauer and Justin Morneau swing from?

9) What term is given to Twins reliever Joe Nathan, who has entered into games in the 9th inning when the Twins are ahead to nail down the win?

10) What position do the following Twins players play: Scott Baker, Nick Blackburn, and Kevin Slowey?

11) How many outs does a team get on defense when they accomplish a "twin-killing"?

12) Two Twins have won an American League Most Valuable Player Award recently and both have the same initials? Who are they?

13) What term or word is used to describe a misplay by the Twins defense?

14) What is the nickname for Twins manager Ron Gardenhire?

15) What does it mean when the "bags are full" or the "sacks are jammed"?

16) If Denard Span is our "lead-off" man, what does that mean?

17) What do they call the "raised" dirt that surrounds the pitching area or the place where the pitcher throws the ball to the plate?

18) What sport did Twins first-baseman Justin Morneau play in the winter in his native Canada?

19) In what two stadiums did the Twins play at least once in a World Series?

20) What Twins player loves to slide head-first on close plays into first-base, even when it isn't necessary or wise to do so?

Justin Morneau

1) T.C. Bear, who came out of hibernation for the 2001 season. T.C. is the grandson of the original bear who starred on the Hamms beer commercials!

2) The Twin Cities of Minneapolis and St. Paul

3) 7

4) Bert Blyleven

5) 7th (7th inning stretch)

6) Visitors. The Twins always bat in the bottom of the inning.

7) Minneapolis. Target Field is just a few Joe Mauer blasts from the Dome.

8) Left-side

9) Closer

10) Pitcher

11) Two. A double play, when two opponents are out on the same play. When the Twins complete a double-play, it really is a Twin-Killing!

12) Joe Mauer (2009) and Justin Morneau (2006)

13) Error

14) Gardy

15) The bases are loaded or a team has a runner on 1st, 2nd, and 3rd bases.

16) It means that he is our first batter up when the Twins bat in the first inning. It can also mean the first batter up in any inning.

17) Mound

18) Hockey. Morneau was a goalie in his native British Columbia.

19) Metropolitan Stadium (Bloomington - 1965) and H.H.H. Metrodome (Minneapolis – 1987 and 1991)

20) Nick Punto

Dan Gladden

8

NAMES AND NICKNAMES

1) What Twins player's last name was a palindrome (word spelled the same forward or backward)?

2) What Twin, a first-baseman from Wisconsin, shares the major-league record for being hit by a pitch three times in one game? (Hint: His nickname was Mongo and he was also a very successful high school baseball coach at Rosemount High School.)

3) What was the nickname of long-time Twins trainer George Lentz?

4) What two Twins, both in the Hall of Fame in Cooperstown, are listed consecutively on the all-time Twins player roster?

5) Jim Hughes, a rookie right-handed starter on the 1975 Minnesota squad, was known as …

6) What Twins left-handed pitcher was referred to as "The Blade"?

7) Catcher "Butch" Wynegar, who started for the Twins at age 20 in 1976, had a given first name of …

8) What last name has been the most common among Twins players from 1961- 2009?

9) What was the other nickname for Ron "Papa Jack" Jackson, a first-baseman and third-basemen from 1979-81? (Hint: he had a propensity to hit the ball high in the air.

10) Of all the 660 players who have competed for the Twins over their 49 years (1961-2009), who has come first and last in the alphabet?

11) What Twins pitcher had the nickname of a baby animal because it fit his last name appropriately?

12) What was the nickname for Twins reliever Juan Berenguer?

13) What Twins left-handed reliever (1990) was called the "Candy Man?

14) What Twins right-handed reliever (1973-76) was known as "Soup"?

15) What was the real first name of Twins designated hitter "Chili" Davis (1991-92)?

16) A trade for this National League catcher would have allowed the Twins to have a battery (pitcher and catcher) with the same names as a morning duo on the Twins flagship radio show in the late 1970's and early 1980's.

17) What was the nickname for Twins outfielder Danny Ford (1975-78), whose personal flair fit the popular musical genre of the era?

18) What Twins reliever who pitched in 1986 and 1987 had the same last name as a famous heavyweight boxer of that era?

19) What Twins infielder possessed the moniker "The Rat"?

20) Francisco Liriano, the lefty starter, is the second person with that last name to play for the Twins. Who was the first?

21) What Twins pitcher (1961-63), a righty reliever, was called "Old Blue"?

22) What smallish left-handed reliever (1961-66) was called, "Shorty"?

23) What Twins catcher and designated hitter, who grew up in the South, was nicknamed "Country" for his accent and upbringing?

24) Besides Frank Quilici, only two other players whose last names start with Q have played in a regular-season game for the Twins. Can you name them?

25) What was popular Twins outfielder "Bombo" Rivera's real first name?

26) What Twins slugger had a six-letter nickname, every letter which was also in his full last name?

27) Twins first baseman Kent Hrbek was a big wrestling fan. What nickname did he go by which had a reference to that sport?

28) What versatile Twins player was tabbed "Pepe", a take-off on his Latino background and his hustling style of play?

29) What present-day Twins coach was one of only two Twins players in history whose last name started with a "U".

30) What long-time *St. Paul Pioneer Press* sports columnist, who pitched briefly for Billy Martin in 1969, was given the nickname...."Shooter"?

31) What is the only name (first and last name) that has been shared by two Twins players? (Hint: they were both catchers.)

32) What is Twins great Tony Oliva's real first name?

33) What was the nickname of Twins reliever Carl Willis?

34) What are the first and middle names of catcher A.J. Pierzynski?

35) Twins pitcher Boof Bonser legally changed his first name after the 2001 season from what?

36) What was the real first name of Chip Hale, a pinch-hitter extraordinaire who also played second base for the Twins (1989-90 and 1993-96)?

37) What Twins outfielder, a key member of two World Series clubs (1987 and 1991) was called "Wrench" for his propensity for dirty uniforms and all-out play?

38) What letter has most commonly started the last name of players on the Twins roster?

39) Who are the only brothers to compete for the Twins?

40) What is the real first name of pitching great Bert Blyleven?

41) What is Harmon Killebrew's middle name?

42) What is the shortest name (first and last names combined) of any Twin?

43) What player's first name is the location of a National League franchise?

44) What has been the most common first name among Twins players?

◀ *Answers to Chapter 8* ▶

1) Mark Salas (Salas). The "Chief" played for the Twins from 1985-87.

2) Craig Kusick. The former first-baseman and designated-hitter played for the Twins from 1973-79. (He was once beaned 3 times in a single game.) Corey Koskie was also beaned three times in a game in 2004.

3) Doc

4) Rod Carew and Steve Carlton

5) Bluegill. Hughes won 16 games as a rookie, still a Twins record.

6) Tom Hall. "The Blade" really was slight; he was 6 feet tall but 150 pounds.

7) Harold.

8) Jackson and Miller. There have been five men named Jackson (Darrell (1978-82); Roy Lee (1986); Mike (2002); Ron (1979-81), and Darrin (1997). The Miller's included: Bob (1968-69), Corky (2005), Damian (1997), Travis (1996-2002), and Jason (2007).

9) Papa-up

10) Paul Abbott (pitcher 1990-92) and Jerry Zimmerman (catcher 1962-68). Close in the alphabet game were Brent Abernathy (2B-2005) and Bill Zepp (RHP-1969-70).

11) Jim Kaat. The popular Twins lefty was called "Kitty" or "Kitty-Kaat."

12) "Senor Smoke." Berenguer was also known as "El Gasolino." Juan had an impressive winning percentage of .717 with a 33-13 mark.

13) John Candelaria, who went 7-3 in 34 games.

14) Bill Campbell. "Soup" led the A.L. in winning percentage (.773) after going 17-5 in 1976, while pitching a whopping 167-⅔ innings of relief that season.

15) Charles

16) Bob Boone. With starting pitcher Roger Erickson (1978-82) already on board, the Twins could have traded for Boone and then had a battery with the the same last names as the popular and talented WCCO morning tandem of Charlie Boone and Roger Erickson.

17) "Disco Dan." The moniker wasn't always considered a compliment to Ford.

18) George Frazier. A right-handed reliever in 1986-87, Frazier gave up Kent Hrbek's first homer at Yankee Stadium in 1981. The boxer, of course, was Joe Frazier.

19) Gary Gaetti. The talented third-sacker, who played for the Twins from 1981-90, had the long, stringy hair in those days.

20) Nelson Liriano. The second baseman played for the team in 1990.

21) Ray Moore, a righthander who pitched in 126 games for the Twins in their first three seasons in Minnesota.

22) Billy Pleis. "Shorty" was only 5'10" and 170 pounds.

23) Matthew LeCroy. The South Carolina product played for the Twins from 2000-2005 and then again in 2007.

24) Tom Quinlan (1996) and Luis Quinones (1992).

25) Jesus. The Puerto Rican native played for the Twins from 1978-80.

26) Harmon Killebrew. His nickname was, of course, "Killer."

27) T Rex

28) Cesar Tovar. The Venezuelan native had an apt moniker.

29) Scott Ullger, who hit just .190 in his one season in 1983.

30) Charley Walters. The Minneapolis native pitched in just 6 games and totaled only 6 innings.

31) Jose Morales. Jose Manuel Morales played for the Twins from 1978-80 and was a super pinch-hitter. A native of the Virgin Islands, he hit .287 over 12 major-league seasons. Jose Guillermo Morales, a native of Puerto Rico, made his Twins debut in 2007 and reappeared in 2009, hitting .328 in 122 at-bats. A second pair, Greg Olson (catcher – 1989) and Gregg Olson (pitcher 1997) differ by only a single letter.

32) Pedro. He was born Pedro Oliva y Lopez on July 20, 1940, in Pinar del Rio, Cuba.

33) "Big Train." Willis was a solid reliever for the Twins from 1991-95, including an 8-3 record and a 2.63 ERA in '91.

34) Anthony John

35) John. Bonser pitched for the Twins from 2006-2008.

36) Walter William. Too bad his last name wasn't Woodrow!

37) Dan Gladden

38) "B". There have been 75 from Wally Backman to Bill Butler. (The letter "M" has had seventy players.)

39) Graig (1967-69) and Jim (1970-72) Nettles

40) Rik Aalbert

41) Clayton

42) Don Lee (pitcher, 1961-62); Joe Lis (first-baseman, 1973-74); and Joe Roa (pitcher, 2004)

43) Houston Jimenez (1983). Actually, Jimenez' first name is really Alfonso and "Houston" is a nickname but became his first name over time.

44) Mike (Michael)

9

TWINS ALL-STARS

1) What person with a Twins connection lost the 1985 All-Star game played at the Metrodome while pitching for another American League team?

2) How many consecutive seasons did Twins infielder Rod Carew earn a spot on the American League All-Star squad?

3) In five different seasons (1962, 1988, 1991, 2001 and 2006) the Twins had two pitchers on the A.L. squad. Who were those hurlers?

4) How many All-Star games did Bloomington native Kent Hrbek play in?

5) Who was the only Twins player to ever win the M.V.P. of the All-Star game?

6) Who are the only native-Minnesotan Twins to be named to an All-Star squad while playing for the Twins?

7) Besides Gary Gaetti, who are the only other Twins to earn an All-Star berth at third-base?

8) What player shares the All-Star game record for most triples in a game with two?

9) Can you name the four Twins to earn All-Star berths as rookies?

10) What Twins catcher was selected to five All-Star teams in the 1960's?

11) How many times did legendary outfielder Kirby Puckett earn the right to play in the All-Star game?

12) How many years was Rod Carew the only Twins representative in the All-Star game?

13) Besides Harmon Killebrew, what other Twins player has hit a homer in the All-Star game?

14) Of Rod Carew's 12 All-Star appearances while with the Twins, how many were earned while playing first-base and how many at second-base?

15) In what year did the Twins have their most representatives in the All-Star game with six and who were they?

Rod Carew

16) Next to Rod Carew (12), what Twins player has appeared most often in the All-Star game (11 appearances)?

17) How many straight seasons did the Twins go without having more than one player represent the team in the A.L. All-Star game?

18) Who is the only Twin to be selected to the All-Star game at three different positions?

19) Who is the only Twins shortstop to play in more than one All-Star game?

20) What player scored the winning run in an A.L. victory the day after winning the home-run derby?

21) What Twins outfielder made a memorable catch on a ball hit by Giants slugger Barry Bonds in Milwaukee in 2002?

22) Who are the only Twins pitchers to start for the A.L. All-Star team?

23) The Twins were the host of the All-Star game on two occasions, once at Metropolitan Stadium and once at the Metrodome. What years did those occur and what was the result?

24) Who is the youngest Twin to ever play in the All-Star game?

25) Joe Mauer has made the All-Star team in the same years that he has won the A.L. batting title. What were those years?

26) How many All-Star games did Twins pitcher Jim Kaat play in?

27) Besides Tony Oliva, Kirby Puckett, and Torii Hunter, only eight other Twins outfielders have ever earned a spot on the A.L. All-Star team in the last 49 years. Who are they?

28) Besides Carew, Killebrew, and Puckett, what Twin has the most All-Star game appearances with eight?

29) Who was the Twins representative in the 1999 All-Star game?

30) Which Twins managers have skippered an A.L. team?

31) What Twins player homered in his home ballpark in the 1965 All-Star game?

32) What Twins outfielder was the only Minnesota player involved in the All-Star game at the Metrodome in 1985?

33) Before Joe Mauer in 2006, who was the last Twins backstop to compete in the Midsummer Classic?

34) What Twins second baseman was picked to be on four All-Star teams in the 1990's?

35) Which two Twins have started an All-Star game at shortstop?

36) Twins righthander Jim Perry won the 1970 A.L. Cy Young award but was he named to the All-Star team during that season?

37) In 1967, the Twins had three starters in the infield for the A.L.; who were they?

38) Which Twin started in the A.L. outfield in 1966?

39) What Twins pitcher made the All-Star team four times in the team's first four seasons in Minnesota?

40) In Rod Carew's dozen appearances in the All-Star game playing as a Twins representative, what was the American League's record?

41) Who was the first Twin' pitcher to make the All-Star team as a reliever?

42) Which Twins have been tagged as the losing pitcher in the All-Star game?

◄ *Answers to Chapter 9* ►

1) Jack Morris. The Highland Park High graduate was the loser in the National League's 6-1 win at the Dome. Morris, pitching for the Detroit Tigers at the time, gave up two runs as the starting pitcher for the A.L.

2) 12. Carew was on the roster in 12 straight All-Star games from 1967-1978 but missed the '70 game due to a knee injury.

3) 1962: Jim Kaat, Camilo Pascual; 1988: Frank Viola, Jeff Reardon; 1991: Jack Morris, Rick Aguilera; 2001: Joe Mays, Eric Milton; 2006: Johan Santana, Fransico Liriano.

4) One. Despite being one of the top first-basemen in the league, Hrbek only played in 1982, his rookie year.

5) Kirby Puckett won the M.V.P. in 1993 at Baltimore's Camden Yards.

6) Kent Hrbek (1982), Jack Morris (1991), and Joe Mauer (2006, 2008, 2009).

7) Rich Rollins (1962) and Harmon Killebrew (1970)

8) Rod Carew. Sir Rodney had two triples on July 11, 1978 at San Diego.

9) Tony Oliva (1964); Rod Carew (1967); Butch Wynegar (1976) and Kent Hrbek (1982)

10) Earl Battey (1962 twice, 1963, 1965, 1966). Joe Mauer has been selected to three All-Star squads (2006, 2008, 2009)

11) 10. Puckett played in all of them consecutively from 1986-1995, (including six as a starter).

12) Four. Carew was the only Twins representative in 1972, 1974, 1975, and 1978.

13) Kirby Puckett (1993) No Twins All-Star other than the "Killer" or "Puck" has ever hit a round-tripper in the All-Star game. Harmon knocked out homers in 1961, 1965, and 1971.

14) 2B-9 times (1967-75) 1B-3 times (1976-78)

15) 1965. The Twins had six players in the "Mid-Summer Classic": Earl Battey, Mudcat Grant, Jimmie Hall, Harmon Killebrew, Tony Oliva, and Zoilo Versalles. (In 1988 the Twins had five: Gary Gaetti, Tim Laudner, Kirby Puckett, Jeff Reardon, and Frank Viola.)

16) Harmon Killebrew. (Kirby Puckett is third with 10).

17) 10. (1978-1987)

18) Harmon Killebrew (3B- 1966, 1969, 1970) (OF- 1963, 1964) (1B- 8 years: 1961 (two games); 1965, 1967, 1968, 1971

19) Zoilo Versalles (1963 and 1965). Other Twins shortstops to earn one berth are Leo Cardenas (1970), Roy Smalley (1979), and Cristian Guzman (2001).

20) Justin Morneau (2008)

21) Torii Hunter, who scaled the fence in right-center field to rob Bonds of a home run.

22) Dean Chance (1967); Frank Viola (1988); Jack Morris (1991).

23) Met Stadium (1965) N.L. 6, A.L. 5; Metrodome (1985) N.L. 6, A.L. 1

24) Butch Wynegar. The York, Pennsylvania product was 20 in 1976.

25) 2006 (.347); 2008 (.328); 2009 (.365).

26) Two. Kaat only pitched in 1962 and 1966.

27) Jimmie Hall (1964-65); Harmon Killebrew (1964); Bob Allison (1963-64); Larry Hisle (1977); Ken Landreaux (1980); Gary Ward (1983); Tom Brunansky (1985) and Matt Lawton (2000).

28) Tony Oliva. The Cuban native played in consecutive All-Star games from 1964-71.

29) Ron Coomer

30) Sam Mele (1966) and Tom Kelly (1988 and 1992)

31) Harmon Killebrew

32) Tom Brunansky

33) A. J. Pierzynski (2002). Mauer was also an All-Star in '08 and 09.

34) Chuck Knoblauch (1992, 1994, 1996, 1997)

35) Zoilo Versalles (1963) and Roy Smalley (1979)

36) Yes. Perry went 24-12 in 1970.

37) Pitcher Dean Chance, first baseman Harmon Killebrew, and second baseman Rod Carew.

38) Tony Oliva

39) Camilo Pascual (1961, 1962 twice, 1964)

40) 1 win and 11 losses. The only victory came in 1971 at Detroit when the A.L. won 6-4 to break an eight-year losing streak.

41) Doug Corbett (1981)

42) Camilo Pascual and Bert Blyleven. The Cuban righthander lost 3-1 in Washington, D.C. on July 10, 1962. It was the first of two All- Star games that season, the other was played at Comiskey Park in Chicago on July 30. For four seasons (1959-62), there were two All-Star games played to help bolster the players' pension funds. Bert, in his only All-Star appearance for the Twins, was the loser in Kansas City on July 24, 1973.

10

MANAGERS AND COACHES

1) In Tom Kelly's 15 full seasons (1987-2001) as Twins manager, in how many seasons did he have a winning record?

2) Who are the five Twins managers who have finished their managing tenure with the club with a winning record?

3) Of the 12 Twins managers, which five served as a player on the team prior to managing the club?

4) Who are the only Twins managers to win an A.L. title or division title in their first full-season as manager?

5) Which Twins managers served as a coach for the team before being named manager?

6) What current Twins coach has served as a coach for 29 consecutive seasons for Minnesota through 2009, serving five different managers?

7) What former Twins pitching coach was the 1955 World Series M.V.P.?

8) Which two Hall of Fame inductees have coached or managed for the Twins?

9) What Twins coach and player helped set a major-league defensive record while playing for the Twins?

10) Which Twins manager once broke up a no-hitter with two outs in the 9th inning of a World Series to win the game for his team?

11) What coach, who served for the Twins from 1986 to 1994, fought on Iwo Jima during WWII?

12) Which Twins manager never played in the major leagues?

13) What was "Cookie" Lavagetto's real first name?

14) What Twins coaches have caught no-hitters in the major leagues?

15) What long-time Twins pitching coach was replaced by Rick Anderson when Tom Kelly retired and Ron Gardenhire took over in 2002 as manager?

16) What former Twins batting coach was named the American League "Player of the Year" by the *Sporting News* in 1965 and 1971? He was a player-coach in his final season (1976) and then served as a coach from 1977-78 and 1985-91.

17) Which Twins manager had the highest career batting average in the major leagues?

18) Tom Kelly finished his final season in 2001 with the Twins with a winning record of 85-77. That season ended a losing streak for the team that totaled how many seasons?

19) Which Twins skipper had his nephew playing a starting role for the team for most of his tenure as the Minnesota manager?

20) Only one Twins manager has won 100 games in a season, and only one has lost 100. Who are they?

21) Which Twins managers wore long sideburns?

22) What former Twins player and coach hit a home run in his first at-bat in the majors?

23) What man was managing the club when it went on a 12-game winning streak in late 1980, only to be dismissed after 37 games in 1981?

24) In what country was present Twins manager Ron Gardenhire born?

25) Which Twins managers had the most career wins and losses, respectively?

26) What current Twins coach was a former teammate of manager

Ron Gardenhire with the New York Mets?

27) What Twins coach was signed by the same Washington Senators scout as his father? A native of Chicago, he was an eleventh-round choice.

28) Which of the team's current coaches also played for the team?

29) Who is the only Twins manager with more than two divisional or league titles?

30) Did Gene Mauch have a winning record as Twins skipper?

31) How many times has Ron Gardenhire been tabbed as American League Manager of the Year?

◀ *Answers to Chapter 10* ▶

1) Tom Kelly (1,140-1,244) had 5 winning seasons and 10 losing seasons.

2) Only five of the 12 Twins managers have had winning records as a Twins manager: Billy Martin (97-65); Sam Mele (522-431); Ron Gardenhire (708-585); Bill Rigney (208-184); and Cal Ermer (145-129).

3) Five Twins managers also played for the Twins: Billy Martin (1961); Billy Gardner (1961); Johnny Goryl (1962-64); Frank Quilici (1965, 1968-71), and Tom Kelly (1975).

4) Billy Martin (1969 A.L. West); Bill Rigney (1970 A.L. West); Tom Kelly (1987 A.L. West, A.L. title, World Series titlist); Ron Gardenhire (2002 A.L. Central).

5) Seven of the 12 Twins managers actually served as a coach: Billy Martin (1965-68); Ron Gardenhire (1991-2001); Billy Gardner (1981); Johnny Goryl (1968-69; 1979-80); Tom Kelly (1983-86); Sam Mele (1961); Frank Quilici (1970-71).

6) Rick Stelmaszek has been a Twins coach since the 1981 season, bridging five different Twins managers from Goryl to Gandenhire.

7) Johnny Podres. He coached the Twins from 1981-85 after winning three games for the Brooklyn Dodgers in their seven-game triumph over the Yankees in 1955.

8) Early Wynn (1967-69); Paul Molitor (2000-01). Wynn was a pitching coach and Molitor was a hitting and baserunning coach.

9) Al Newman, who was a coach from 2002 to 2005. The backup second baseman was in on the triple plays with both Gary Gaetti and Kent Hrbek when Jody Reed and Tom Brunansky bounced into the 5-4-3 triples plays at Boston on July 17, 1990.

10) "Cookie" Lavagetto. The Brooklyn Dodger pinch-hitter smacked a double off the wall to knock in two runs, including the game-winner as the Dodgers won 3-2. Lavagetto's hit was the only hit given up by the Yanks' Bill Bevens in Game 4 of the 1947 World Series. The Yanks' won the Series 4-3.

11) Wayne "Twig" Terwilliger. "Twig" was a vital resource on the Twins two world champion clubs.

12) Ray Miller. Cal Ermer (1967-1968) only played in one game for the Senators in 1947 and went 0-3 at the plate.

13) Harry.

14) Bob Rodgers and Jerry Zimmerman

15) Dick Such. Tom Kelly's right-hand man was on the staff for 17 seasons (1985-2001).

16) Tony Oliva.

17) Cookie Lavagetto. The former Brooklyn Dodger and Pittsburgh Pirate third-baseman hit .269 during his 10-year career. He barely beats out his successor as manager, Sam Mele, who hit .267 in his own 10-year career as an outfielder during the same era.

18) Eight. The Twins were a combined 528-699 from 1993-2000 for a lowly winning percentage of .430. Now, that's called job security!

19) Gene Mauch. Twins shortstop Roy Smalley was the son of Mauch's sister. Smalley played two stints with the club (1976-82 and 1985-87) and still ranks 10th all-time in Twins history in hits, runs-batted-in, at-bats, and games played and finished with a .262 average in 10 seasons.

20) Sam Mele won 102 games for the American League pennant winners in 1965 while Billy Gardner's 1982 club went 60-102.

21) Ray Miller and Frank Quilici. While a highly-successful pitching coach, Miller fared poorly as a manager with Minnesota. He was 109-130 after replacing Billy Gardner in 1985 before being succeeded himself by Tom Kelly late in 1986. Quilici was 280-287 from 1972-75 and his long and wide sideburns fit the era.

22) Rick Renick. The third-baseman hit his first homer for the Twins on July 11, 1968.

23) Johnny Goryl. The former Twins infielder had managed 36 games after replacing Gene Mauch in August, 1981 and went 23-13. His team was just 11-25 when owner Calvin Griffith put Billy Gardner in his spot.

24) West Germany. "Gardy" was born on Oct. 24, 1957, in what was then called West Germany as his father was stationed in the military there. (Germany was divided at the end of WWII, and East and West Germany were separate nations until reunified in 1990.)

25) Tom Kelly and Tom Kelly. He won 1,140 games in his 15-year tenure but also lost 1,244 contests for a winning percentage of .478%

26) Rick Anderson (pitcher)

27) Rick Stelmaszek. The scout was Jack Sheehan. "Stelly" hit .170 in three seasons for four different teams from 1971-74.

28) Scott Ullger. He played in 35 games, hitting just .190 as a first-baseman in 1983. Ironically, Ullger served as the Twins batting coach for eight years!

29) Ron Gardenhire. "Gardy" won A.L. Central titles in his first three seasons (20002, 2003, 2004) and went on to win two others in 2006 and 2009.

30). No. Mauch had a losing record of 378-394 (.490) from 1976-80.

31) None. However, Gardenhire was second in the voting for A.L. Manager of the Year on no less than five occasions. In 2003, 2004, 2006, 2008, and 2009 Gardy finished second, a true testament to his respect in baseball circles. Ron also finished third in his first season (2002). Gardenhire has the most second-place finishes in A.L. history. Tony LaRussa has been runner-up six times but some of his have come in the NL. LaRussa has won four overall titles.

11

NATIVE-MINNESOTANS AS MINNESOTA TWINS

Twenty-seven players who were born in Minnesota have played for the Twins. Can you match the player with his birthplace? (Note: some locations apply to more than one player, others to none.)

___1). Fred Bruckbauer	A.	Hermantown
___2). Dave Winfield	B.	Faribault
___3). Dick Stigman	C.	Alexandria
___4). Paul Molitor	D.	St. Paul
___5). Jerry Terrell	E.	Lamberton
___6). Charley Walters	F.	Winona
___7). Jerry Koosman	G.	Graceville
___8). Mike Mason	H.	Minneapolis
___9). Dave Goltz	I.	Pelican Rapids
__10). Greg Olson	J.	Waseca
__11). Mike Poepping	K.	Bemidji
__12). Tom Quinlan	L.	Duluth
__13). Kent Hrbek	M.	Brooklyn Park
__14). Paul Giel	N.	New Ulm
__15). Tom Kelly	O.	Taconite
__16). Bob Gebhard	P.	Little Falls
__17). Michael Restovich	Q.	Grand Rapids
__18). Joe Mauer	R.	Willow River
__19). Brian Raabe	S.	Nimrod
__20). Tom Burgmeier	T.	Appleton
__21). Glen Perkins	U.	Richfield
__22). Terry Steinbach	V.	St. Cloud
__23). Jerry Kindall	W.	Marshall
__24). Jim Eisenreich	X.	Albany
__25). Tom Johnson	Y.	Austin
__26). Jack Morris	Z.	Rochester
__27). George Thomas		

Native Minnesotan Jerry Kindall

◀ Answers to Chapter 11 ▶

1)	N	10)	W	19)	N
2)	D	11)	P	20)	D
3)	S	12)	D	21)	D
4)	D	13)	H	22)	N
5)	J	14)	F	23)	D
6)	H	15)	G	24)	V
7)	T	16)	E	25)	D
8)	B	17)	Z	26)	D
9)	I	18)	D	27)	H

12

NON-PLAYING PERSONNEL

1) The Twins' long-time minor-league director was signed by the Washington Senators after an impressive pitching career for the NCAA champion Minnesota Gophers in 1960. Who is he?

2) When Twins' long-time public-address announcer Bob Casey died on March 27, 2005, at age 79 after working more than 3,500 major-league games in 44 seasons, who took his place?

3) Who was the Twins equipment manager in the 1960's who opened up a baseball museum and souvenir shop near the Metrodome?

4) Who were the two primary physicians for the Twins for the first two decades of their existence in Minnesota?

5) What is the hometown of veteran Twins TV broadcaster Dick Bremer, a native-Minnesotan?

6) Prior to joining the Twins in time to broadcast the magical 1987 season, John Gordon had broadcast games for what two other American League teams?

7) The broadcast booth at the Metrodome is named in honor of what Twins Hall of Fame broadcaster?

8) What Twins broadcaster used the following line to let listeners know that a Twins player had just homered: "You Can Wave It Bye-Bye"?

9) How many different partners did Herb Carneal have in his long career announcing games on the radio for the Twins?

10) What long-time WCCO radio announcer for the Gopher football and basketball teams shared broadcasts with Carneal for four years in the early 1970's?

11) Who serves as the color analyst on the Spanish language broadcasts on the Twins radio network on KMNV (1470)?

12) Halsey Hall, the former Twin Cities sportswriter who worked color commentary from 1961 to 1972, was famous for what phrase while on the air?

13) What Twin Cities television station broadcast games from the team's arrival in Minnesota in 1961 until 1972?

14) What Twins public-relations director, who also served a long tenure as the official scorer at Twins games, also worked "color commentary" on games in 1992 and 1993?

15) Herb Carneal, the long-time voice of the Twins radio broadcast who won the Ford C. Frick award from the Baseball Hall of Fame in 1996, worked games for the Twins for how many years?

16) Besides Jerry Bell and Dave St. Peter, what three sons of former owner Carl Pohlad are on the team's present executive board?

17) What special title do former Twin greats Rod Carew, Kent Hrbek, Harmon Killebrew, and Tony Oliva now have with the ballclub?

18) Who are the only Twins front-office personnel to be named "Executive of the Year" for Major League Baseball?

19) What scout signed Twins legend Kirby Puckett?

20) What was Herb Carneal's trademark greeting to fans when he started each baseball broadcast?

21) Bob Casey, the venerable public-address announcer, also worked for the Vikings for a short period during the 1960's. In 1963, what infamous remark did he make in describing an infraction by an opponent?

22) Who is the first woman to serve as the official public-address announcer for a Twins game?

23) What Twins color-man once started his sport-coat on fire and enjoyed smoking cigars and chomping on onions?

24) Which Hockey Hall of Fame member shared the WCCO radio broadcast booth with Herb Carneal, Ray Christensen, and Halsey Hall in 1970?

25) For how many seasons, did Hall of Fame broadcaster Herb Carneal work major-league baseball?

26) Who replaced Terry Ryan as the Twins general manager following the 2007 season?

27) Who is the current president of the Minnesota Twins? (Hint: He is the father of a set of "twins" himself.)

28) Who was the director of scouting who drafted and signed many of the players who played on the Twins' 1987 championship team?

29) What minor-league team, as of 2010, is closest to Minnesota?

30) Along with Calvin Griffith and Carl Pohlad, what Twins executive threw out the so-called "first pitch" before Game 7 of the 1987 World Series?

31) What former major-league manager and World Series winner did the Twins hire prior to the 1987 season to help general manager Andy MacPhail and first-year manager Tom Kelly in evaluating talent during spring training?

32) When Carl Pohlad officially took over the Twins club on September 7, 1984, it put an end to the Griffith family's control of the ballclub. How many years did the Griffith family own the franchise?

33) What jobs did the father and grandfather of former Twins general manager Andy McPhail hold in baseball?

34) What television broadcasters have worked play-by-play for both the local NHL team and the major-league baseball club?

35) When the Washington Senators' decided to move to Minnesota, who was the first Minnesotan hired by the franchise to expedite the move to the Twin Cities?

36) What is the home-run call of veteran Twins play-by-play broadcaster John Gordon (1987-2009)?

◀ *Answers to Chapter 12* ▶

1) Jim Rantz. Rantz never made it to the big leagues but he was named to the Twins Hall of Fame in 2007 for his contributions to the team.

2) Bob Kurtz. The voice of the Minnesota Wild on WCCO radio, Kurtz has previously broadcast Twins games on TV from 1979-86.

3) Ray Crump

4) Dr. Leonard Michienzi and Dr. Harvey O'Phelan.

5) Staples. Bremer has broadcast games for the Twins since 1983, beginning with Spectrum Sports TV. He now appears on Fox Sports Net.

6) Baltimore Orioles and New York Yankees

7) Herb Carneal. Herb, who died on April 1, 2007, at age 83, joined the Twins in 1962 and broadcast games in five different decades. He did broadcasts in Philadelphia for both the A's and Phillies in 1954 and then worked Baltimore Orioles broadcasts from 1957 to 1961. In 1996, Herb received the Ford Frick Award from the Baseball Hall of Fame.

8) Joe Angel. He broadcast games for three seasons (1984-86). A native of Columbia, he is famous for pronouncing the names of Latin players correctly, and has also broadcast games for the Yankees, Marlins, Orioles, Giants, and A's.

9) 17

10) Ray Christensen

11) Tony Oliva

12) "Holy Cow"

13) WTCN. In 1973, WCCO-TV earned the broadcast rights until WTCN won them back in 1975.

14) Tom Mee

15) 44. Carneal started with the Twins in 1962 and worked through the 2006 season, although he did just homes games in the final years due to frail health.

16) Jim, Bill, and Bob Pohlad

17) Special Assistant

18) Calvin Griffith (1965), Andy MacPhail (1991) and Terry Ryan (2002, 2006) were all honored by *The Sporting News* and Ryan was named "Executive of the Year" by Baseball America in 2004.

19) Ellsworth Brown. Puckett was signed in the 3rd round of the winter draft in 1982.

20) "Hi, everybody"

21) "The Giants have been penalized 15 yards for having an illegitimate man on the field." Casey was infamous for his malaprops but overall did an outstanding job for the Twins.

22) Kim Jeffries. The WCCO radio personality was subbing for Bob Casey, as he was in Cooperstown, New York for Kirby Puckett's enshrinement in the Hall of Fame on Aug.5, 2001.

23) Halsey Hall

24) Al Shaver. The former Minnesota North Star broadcaster and their only play-by-play man during their tenure in the Twin Cities (1967-93) worked Twins games for just that one season. Ray Christensen, of course, was also a WCCO employee and Ray worked four seasons (1970-73) doing Twins broadcasts.

25) 50. Carneal was voted into the Twins Hall of Fame in 2001.

26) Bill Smith.

27) Dave St. Peter, a native of Bismarck, North Dakota. His twin sons are named Eric and Ben.

28) George Brophy, who was elected to the Twins Hall of Fame in 2009.

29) Beloit, Wisconsin. The Snappers play in the Class A Midwest League.

30) Howard Fox.

31) Ralph Houk, the former New York Yankee, Detroit Tiger, and Boston Red Sox manager. Houk spent 20 years as a skipper in the A.L. and won two world titles with the Yankees (1961 and 1962).

32) 72 years. Calvin Griffith's uncle Clark owned the team from 1920 to 1955 after managing four teams, including the Senators, from 1912 to 1920. Calvin took over when Clark died in 1955.

33) Andy MacPhail's father Lee was President of the American League and his grandfather Larry was the chief executive officer for three teams (Brooklyn Dodgers, Cincinnati Reds, and New York Yankees). Andy himself was the Twins General Manager from 1985 to 1994. Lee and Larry are the only father-and-son members of the Baseball Hall of Fame.

34) Bob Kurtz (Minnesota North Stars and Minnesota Wild); Joe Boyle (Minnesota North Stars); Dick Bremer (Minnesota North Stars); Frank Buetel (Minnesota North Stars).

35) Tom Mee, who was first employed as an assistant public-relations director before becoming the Director of Public Relations a few years later. Mee retired in 1991.

36) "Touch 'Em All"

13

TWINS AWARDS AND HONORS

1) Who is the only Twins player to share an American League Rookie of the Year award with another player?

2) In what years did Tom Kelly win the A.L. Manager of the Year award?

3) Who was the first Twins hurler to win the American League Cy Young award?

4) Five Twins have won the A.L. Most Valuable Player award. Which positions did they play?

5) What Twins player never won an A.L. Most Valuable Player award but finished second twice and fourth once?

6) On two occasions, a Twins player has earned the Outstanding Designated Hitter award by the American League. Who were they?

7) Kirby Puckett never won a MVP trophy. How many times did he finish either second or third in the voting?

8) Who are the only Twins players to win the A.L. Championship Series Most Valuable Player award?

9) Lefthander Johan Santana won the Cy Young award for the A. L. twice. In what years did the Venezuelan native win them?

10) What Panama native won the A.L. Rookie-of-the-Year award in 1967 after hitting .292?

11) The only two Twins to win the World Series Most Valuable Player award were pitchers. Who were they?

12) In 1977, what Twins infielder won the A.L. MVP award after knocking in 100 runs and totaling 14 homers, both career highs? (Hint: He also flirted with hitting .400, finishing at .388.)

13) In 1995, what Twins outfielder became the fifth for the club to win the Rookie-of-the-Year award after clubbing 24 home runs and knocking in 84 runs?

14) Who aced out Jim Kaat for the 1966 Cy Young award?

15) Which Twins slugger was tabbed as the 1969 American League Most Valuable Player after knocking in 140 runs and swatting 49 homers?

16) What Twin became the A.L. Most Valuable Player without hitting more than 20 homers, without batting at least .300, and without knocking in at least 100 runs?

17) In 2006, what Canadian native won the A.L. Most Valuable Player award as a Twin?

18) In 1998 the *Sporting News* named the top 100 players in baseball history. Which Twins were included on that list?

19) Which Twins star won the Gold Glove award 12 straight times?

20) Besides Johan Santana, who is the only other Twins lefthander to win a Cy Young award?

21) Which of the following players won the Rookie-of-the-Year award as Twins players: Kent Hrbek, Chuck Knobluach, or Joe Mauer?

22) In the Twins original Hall of Fame class of 2000, six persons were honored and one was a non-player, former owner Calvin Griffith. Who were the legendary players?

23) Which three Twins have won the Roberte Clemente award, given by Major League Baseball to the player who best exemplifies the game of baseball, sportsmanship, community involvement, and individual contributions to the team?

24) Who was the first Twins player to win the A.L. Rookie of the Year award in 1964, to this day one of the most outstanding all-around years by a rookie in major-league history?

Johan Santana

25) What non-pitchers have won at least four Gold Glove awards for the Minnesota Twins?

26) Can you name the individuals, other than Calvin Griffith, to be admitted to the Twins Hall of Fame as non-players?

27) Which player has won the Most Valuable Twin award as selected by the Twin Cities Baseball Writers the most times?

28) Which Twins relievers have won the Fireman of the Year or the Rolaids Relief Award in the American League?

29) What Twins players have been selected as the Most Improved Twin by local media members in consecutive seasons?

30) Each year, the Twin Cities Baseball Writers choose the Upper Midwest Player of the Year, which means any player from the north-central region of the country on any team in the majors. Which Twins player is the only one to win it more than once?

31) Who was voted the team's top pitcher by the local media five straight seasons?

32) What Twins player was the 1967 A.L "Comeback Player of the Year"?

33) The Twins have two members on the current team who have won the "Minor League Player of the Year" award? Who are they?

34) What Twins hitter has won the most Silver Slugger awards, given to the player at each position in each league who had the best offensive season?

35) What Twins player got 27 of 28 first-place votes to easily win the 2009 A.L. Most Valuable Player award?

36) Who are the three players to be enshrined into the Baseball Hall of Fame in Cooperstown at a younger age than Kirby Puckett?

1) John Castino. The Twins third-baseman shared it with Toronto shortstop Alfredo Griffin in 1979.

2) 1987 and 1991. In both of those season, the Twins won the A.L. Western Division title, the American League pennant, and the World Series.

3) Jim Perry (1970). Gaylord's older brother went 24-12 with a 3.04 ERA.

4) Zoilo Versalles (1965, shortstop), Joe Mauer (2009, catcher), Justin Morneau (2006, 1st base), Rod Carew (1977, 1st base) and Harmon Killebrew (1969, 80 games at 1st and 108 at 3rd).

5) Tony Oliva, who finished second in 1965 and 1970 and fourth in 1964.

6) Chili Davis (1991) and Paul Molitor (1996)

7) Puckett was second in MVP voting in 1992 and third twice (1987 and 1988). Kirby was in the top ten in MVP votes an impressive seven times in his 12-year career (1984-1995)

8) Gary Gaetti (1987) and Kirby Puckett (1991)

9) 2004 and 2006

10) Rod Carew. After hitting .273 in his second season, Carew would go on to hit at least .300 for 10 straight seasons for the team. Sir Rodney won seven batting titles during that time, including four occasions when he hit .350 or better.

11) Frank Viola (1987) and Jack Morris (1991)

12) Rod Carew. Sir Rodney's .388 average that year was the highest since Ted Williams hit .388 in 1958.

13) Marty Cordova

14) Sandy Koufax. The Dodger great went 27-9 with a 1.73 ERA to win the award, which was given to the outstanding pitcher in the majors overall, the final such season it was awarded in this fashion.

15) Harmon Killebrew. The "gentleman" basher ended up leading the A.L. in homers for the fifth time and home-run percentage for the sixth time as a Twin.

16) Zoilo Versalles. The shortstop won the 1965 M.V.P. award for his all-around play on both offense and defense. That year he had 19 homers, batted .273, and had 73 RBIs.

17) Justin Morneau. The British Columbia-born Morneau hit .321, slugged 34 homers, and knocked in 130 runs.

18) Rod Carew (61st), Harmon Killebrew (69th), Kirby Puckett (86th) and Paul Molitor (99th).

19) Jim Kaat. "Kitty" won from 1962 to 1972 for the Twins, and won again the next year when he pitched for both the Twins and White Sox. He went on to win four more in his 25-year pitching career. Outfielder Torii Hunter won seven straight Gold Gloves from 2001 to 2007.

20) Frank Viola. The St. John's, New York college star won 24 games and had a 2.64 ERA and struck out 193 batters to earn the award in 1988.

21) Chuck Knoblauch. The Texas A & M product won the 1991 award and batted leadoff for the '91 World Series titlists. Hrbek was second to the Orioles' Cal Ripken in 1982 and Mauer was hurt for most of his rookie year in 2004 and wasn't a factor in the voting.

22) Rod Carew, Harmon Killebrew, Kent Hrbek, Tony Oliva, and Kirby Puckett, each of whom have had their numbers retired by the club.

23) Rod Carew (1977), Dave Winfield (1994), and Kirby Puckett (1996).

24) Tony Oliva. The Cuban immigrant led the league in hitting (.323), total bases (374), and hits (217) and also slugged 32 homers.

25) Kirby Puckett (1986-89, 91-92) and Torii Hunter (2001-2007) won six and seven, respectively, as outfielders and Gary Gaetti (1986-89) won four straight at third base.

26) Broadcaster Herb Carneal (2001); manager Tom Kelly (2002); public-address announcer Bob Casey (2003): owner Carl Pohlad (2005); farm director Jim Rantz (2007), and front-office employee George Brophy (2009).

27) Rod Carew and Kirby Puckett, both six times.

28) Ron Perranoski was the *Sporting News* Fireman of the Year in 1969 and 1970; Mike Marshall was co-winner (with Jim Kern) of the same award in 1979, and Jeff Reardon was co-winner with Dave Righetti in 1987. Bill Campbell won the Rolaids Relief Man Award in 1976.

29) Ted Uhlaender (1968-69) and Cesar Tovar (1970-71). Jim Kaat, Mark Guthrie, and Carlos Silva all won twice, but not consecutively.

30) Joe Mauer (2006, 2008, and 2009). Paul Molitor won it seven times but just once (1996) as a Twin. Jack Morris won it four times but just once (1991) with Minnesota.

31) Johan Santana (2003-2007)

32) Dean Chance

33) Joe Mauer (2003) and Francisco Liriano (2005). Matt Garza, a former Twins hurler traded to Tampa Bay, also won in 2006 as a farmhand.

34) Kirby Puckett. The "Puck" won six times (1986-89, 1992, 1994).

35) Joe Mauer, who led the majors in batting (.365) and led the A.L. in on-base percentage and slugging percentage, in addition to clubbing 28 homers and totaling 96 RBI.

36) Lou Gehrig (36), Sandy Koufax (36), and Roberto Clemente (38). Puckett was 40 years old when he was announced as an entrant but was 41 by the time he was officially enshrined on Aug. 5, 2001, along with former Twins player Dave Winfield. Puckett, born on March 14, 1960, is the first player to be inducted into the Hall of Fame who was born in the 1960's.

14

UNIFORM NUMBERS

Following is a list of some of the top players in Twins history. Please mark the uniform number worn by each player through all or most of his career. A few players wore more than one number for more than a few seasons so some players will require more than one number. Mark the numbers that are now retired by the Twins with an asterisk.

_____ Kirby Puckett	_____ Jeff Reardon
_____ Harmon Killebrew	_____ Rod Carew
_____ Tony Oliva	_____ Johan Santana
_____ Kent Hrbek	_____ Joe Mauer
_____ Justin Morneau	_____ Bert Blyleven
_____ Francisco Liriano	_____ Jim Kaat
_____ Earl Battey	_____ Zoilo Versalles
_____ Frank Viola	_____ Gary Gaetti
_____ Rick Aguilera	_____ Camilo Pascual
_____ Torii Hunter	_____ Bob Allison
_____ Jim Perry	_____ Cesar Tovar
_____ Jack Morris	_____ Corey Koskie
_____ Michael Cuddyer	_____ Roy Smalley
_____ Brad Radke	_____ Tom Brunansky
_____ Jim Grant	_____ Dan Gladden
_____ Chuck Knoblauch	_____ Larry Hisle
_____ Paul Molitor	_____ Dave Winfield
_____ Don Mincher	_____ Butch Wynegar

____ Eddie Guardado	____ A.L. Worthington
____ Brian Harper	____ Juan Berenguer
____ Rich Rollins	____ Jacque Jones
____ Jim Merritt	____ Jimmie Hall
____ Joe Nathan	____ Bobby Darwin
____ Ron Perranoski	____ Jack Kralick
____ Dick Stigman	____ Dean Chance
____ Dave Goltz	____ Marty Cordova
____ John Castino	____ Lyman Bostock
____ A. J. Pierzynski	____ Vic Power
____ Ted Uhlaender	____ Danny Ford
____ Mickey Hatcher	____ Rich Reese
____ Scott Erickson	____ Dave Engle
____ Lenny Green	____ Jerry Koosman
____ Chili Davis	____ Kenny Landreaux
____ Shane Mack	____ David Ortiz
____ Jerry Terrell	____ Geoff Zahn
____ Shannon Stewart	____ Mike Cubbage
____ LaTroy Hawkins	____ Mike Marshall
____ Nick Punto	____ Mike Pagliarulo
____ Rob Wilfong	____ Tom Hall
____ Gene Larkin	____ Bernie Allen
____ Allan Anderson	____ Johnny Roseboro
____ Leo Cardenas	____ Billy Pleis
____ Terry Steinbach	____ Matt Lawton
____ Kevin Slowey	____ Gary Ward
____ Bill Tuttle	____ Tom Burgmeier

____	Randy Bush	____	Steve Braun
____	Tim Laudner	____	Billy Martin
____	Tom Kelly	____	Tim Teufel
____	Ron Davis	____	Kevin Tapani
____	Carlos Gomez	____	Scott Baker
____	Scott Leius	____	Steve Brye
____	Pete Redfern	____	Jerry Zimmerman
____	Greg Gagne	____	Ron Washington
____	Eric Milton	____	Mike Smithson
____	Mike Redmond	____	Lew Ford
____	Roger Erickson	____	Glenn Borgmann
____	Al Newman	____	Steve Lombardozzi
____	Luis Rivas	____	Mark Guthrie
____	Joe Mays	____	Kyle Lohse
____	Bill Campbell	____	Ron Coomer
____	Joe Decker	____	Jim Hughes
____	Tom Johnson	____	Glenn Adams
____	Pedro Munoz	____	Delmon Young
____	Paul Molitor	____	Juan Rincon
____	Bob Wells	____	Carl Willis
____	Carlos Silva	____	Matt Guerrier
____	Denard Span	____	Jason Kubel
____	Pat Neshek	____	Doug Mientkiewicz
____	Mike Trombley	____	Dave Boswell
____	Cristian Guzman		

Number   Player(s)

1   Jerry Terrell, Billy Martin (also, manager)

2   Zoilo Versalles, John Castino, Bobby Darwin, Luis Rivas, Denard Span, Bernie Allen

3   Harmon Killebrew (retired number)*

4   Bob Allison, Steve Braun, Steve Lombardozzi, Paul Molitor

5   Roy Smalley, Michael Cuddyer, Don Mincher, Danny Thompson, Pedro Munoz

6   Tony Oliva (retired number) *

7   Joe Mauer, Greg Gagne, Lenny Green, Rob Wilfong, Jimmie Hall, Jerry Terrell

8   Gary Gaetti, Nick Punto, Ron Coomer, Glenn Adams

9   Rich Rollins, Larry Hisle, Mickey Hatcher, Gene Larkin

10   Earl Battey, Lyman Bostock, Tom Kelly (also, manager)

11   Chuck Knoblauch, Jacque Jones, Ted Uhlaender, Steve Brye, Tim Teufel

12   Cesar Tovar, Brian Harper, Bernie Allen

13   Bill Tuttle, Johnny Roseboro, Mike Pagliarulo

14   Kent Hrbek (retired number) *, Glenn Borgmann

15   Danny Ford, Jack Kralick, Al Worthington, Tim Laudner, Cristian Guzman

16   Frank Viola, Butch Wynegar, Doug Mientkiewicz, Ron Perranoski, Jason Kubel

17   Camilo Pascual, Leo Cardenas, Pete Redfern, Pat Neshek

18   Eddie Guardado, Dick Stigman

19   Scott Erickson, Roger Erickson, Billy Pleis, Tom Burgmeier

20   Rich Reese, Dave Engle, Lew Ford

21   Tom Hall, Mike Trombley, Delmon Young, Joe Decker, Tom Johnson

22   Brad Radke, Carlos Gomez, Jerry Zimmerman

23   Dave Boswell, Shannon Stewart

24   Tom Brunansky, Shane Mack, Bill Campbell

25   Randy Bush, Joe Mays

26   A.J. Pierzynski, Jim Merritt, Mike Cubbage, Al Newman

27   David Ortiz

28   Bert Blyleven, Vic Power, Mike Marshall

29   Rod Carew (retired number) *

30   Dave Goltz, Scott Baker, Jimmie Hall

31   Jim Perry, Greg Gagne, Scott Leius, Jim Hughes

32   Dan Gladden, Dean Chance, Dave Winfield, LaTroy Hawkins, Tom Johnson, Gary Ward

33   Justin Morneau, Jim Grant

34   Kirby Puckett (retired number) *

36   Jim Kaat, Joe Nathan, Jerry Koosman, Kevin Tapani, Terry Steinbach

38   Rick Aguilera, Geoff Zahn, Ron Washington

39   Ron Davis, Juan Rincon

40   Marty Cordova, Juan Berengeur

41   Jeff Reardon, Eric Milton

42   (Jackie Robinson) ** Retired by major-league directive

44   Ken Landreaux, Chili Davis

46   Bob Wells

47   Francisco Liriano, Corey Koskie, Jack Morris

48   Torii Hunter, Mike Smithson

49   Allan Anderson, Kyle Lohse

50   Matt Lawton

51   Carl Willis

52   Carlos Silva

53   Mark Guthrie

54   Matt Guerrier

55   Mike Redmond

57   Johan Santana

59   Kevin Slowey

Torii Hunter

15

STADIUMS AND THE PLAYING FIELD

1) In what year was ground broken for the construction of Metropolitan Stadium in Bloomington?

2) What team was the first tenant at Metropolitan Stadium, taking up residence between 1956 and 1960, and which of its managers during that stint later managed the Twins?

3) In what stadium did the Twins have a better overall winning percentage, Met Stadium or the Metrodome?

4) How many blocks is it from the Metrodome to Target Field?

5) Who were the Twins opponents in their first games at Met Stadium, the Metrodome, and Target Field?

6) What type of rock is exposed on the exterior of Target Field?

7) The highest attendance for any Twins home game came on Oct. 9, 2002, when the Twins lost to the Angels 6-3 in the A.L. Championship Series. What was the attendance that day?

8) What was the distance to the center-field fence at Met Stadium?

9) On June 3, 1967 Harmon Killebrew smashed his legendary 520-foot homer into the upper deck in left field at the old Met. What Angels pitcher, a former World Series hero with the Milwaukee Braves, gave up the homer?

10) From 1961-81, who served as the Twins' head groundskeeper at Met Stadium?

11) Which side of the field did the Twins use as their home dugout at Metropolitan Stadium and the Metrodome? Which side will be their home dugout at Target Field?

12) What are the addresses of the Metrodome and Target Field?

13) What hotel/motels were located adjacent to Metropolitan Stadium?

14) Where were the bullpens located originally at Met Stadium?

15) In what year was air-conditioning installed at the Metrodome?

16) What were the three different field substances or turfs that were installed in the Metrodome?

17) What unique feature will Target Field possess along the 5th Street side of the ballpark, in a true effort to connect to the past?

18) What were the three ticket prices at Metropolitan Stadium in 1961?

19) In what year did the Twins start playing games in downtown Minneapolis at the Metrodome?

20) The Metrodome, which was named for former Minneapolis mayor, U.S. Senator, and Vice-President Hubert H. Humphrey. What was Hubert's middle name?

21) What two cities and ballparks have hosted the most northerly World Series games?

22) In what year was Metropolitan Stadium demolished?

23) What were the approximate construction costs for Metropolitan Stadium, the H.H.H. Metrodome, and Target Field?

24) The Metrodome is the only facility in the United States to haved served as a venue for all of what four major sporting events?

25) Met Stadium was bounded by Cedar Avenue on the west, 24th Avenue South on the south, East 83rd Street on the east, and 83rd Street on the north. What was 83rd Street later changed to?

26) What is the smallest attendance for any home game in Twins history?

27) What part of Met Stadium is to be utilized at the new "Target Field" in 2010?

28) The earliest date that the Twins ever opened their home season at Met Stadium came on what date in 1971?

29) In what year did the Twins attract an astounding 37,416 fans per game at the Metrodome?

30) Have the Twins ever averaged less than 10,000 fans per home game for any year of their existence?

31) What will be the official capacity for Target Field?

32) What fabric was the Metrodome's roof comprised of?

33) What was the average "Opening Day" temperature for the 21 (1961-81) openers at Met Stadium?

34) The warmest temperature for a Twins opener at Met Stadium occurred on April 22, 1980 when the temperature at gametime was...

35) What is the height of the right-field wall at Target Field?

36) The Metrodome includes 7,600 retractable seats in rightfield, the largest such section of any stadium in the world. How long does it take to convert from baseball to football or vice-versa?

37) What was the term used by many people, especially those not from the Upper Midwest, for the H.H.H. Metrodome in its early existence?

38) For what purpose did approximately 15,000 fans show up for a baseball-related event on March 12, 2006 at the Metrodome, despite the winter's worst storm?

39) What architectural firm designed Target Field?

40) Who played at Met Stadium on August 21, 1965, in front of a crowd of approximately 30,000 fans?

41) How did starting pitcher Jim Kaat arrive at Met Stadium for Opening Day on April 12, 1965?

1) 1955. Construction began on June 25 that year and concluded less than a year later at a cost of $4.5 million, financed by revenue bonds. The 160 acres of land were purchased at a cost of $2, 980 per acre. Met Stadium was ready for the American Association season on April 24, 1956.

2) The Minneapolis Millers. Their manager for the 1958 and 1959 seasons was future Twins manager Gene Mauch.

3) Met Stadium. In 1,669 total games at Metropolitan Stadium, the Twins went 910-759 for a winning percentage of .545. In the Metrodome, through the 2009 season, Minnesota was 1,214-1,028 for a .541 winning percentage. The Twins played a total of 2,242 games at the Metrodome. All told, the Twins are 2,124-1,787 at home in their history in Minnesota for an overall winning percentage of .543 in 3,911 games.

4) Twelve blocks.

5) Met Stadium – April 21, 1961 versus Washington; Metrodome – April 6, 1982 versus Seattle; Target Field – April 12, 2010 versus Boston

6) Native Minnesota limestone quarried near Mankato.

7) 55, 990.

8) It varied; 412 ft (1961); 430 (1965); 425 (1968); 410 (1975); 402 (1977)

9) Lew Burdette

10) Dick Ericson

11) First base side at Met Stadium; third base side at Metrodome, and first base side at Target Field.

12) 34 Kirby Puckett Place for the Metrodome and 1 Twins Way, 290 7th St N. for Target Field.

13) Thunderbird Motel, Marriott Hotel, Howard Johnsons, and the Registry Hotel.

14) Behind the right-center field and right field fences. Later, they were moved adjacent to the left field and right field foul lines.

15) 1983 (The first game played with air conditioning was June 28.)

16) Super-Turf, also called SporTurf, was the original surface from 1982-86. In 1987, AstroTurf replaced it. In 2004, another surface called FieldTurf, was installed.

17) There will be multiple "Knotholes" along the wall in order to allow fans to watch the action on the field without buying a ticket.

18) $3 for box seats, $2.50 for reserved seats, and $1.50 for general admission. (Believe it or not, the prices stayed exactly the same for the first seven seasons, 1961-67!)

19) 1982. The author has four seats from the Met in his basement; they were located between home plate and third base in the lower deck!

20) Horatio

21) Met Stadium in Bloomington, Minnesota (1965) and the Metrodome in Minneapolis (1987 and 1991). Toronto (1992 and 1993) lies 1 degree latitude south of both Minnesota cities.

22) 1985

23) $8.5 million for Met Stadium, $68 million for the Metrodome, and $545 million for Target Field. (That includes $390 million to built the ballpark itself and the rest for enhancements and infrastructure.)

24) The Metrodome is the only venue to host a major-league All-Star game (1985), a Super Bowl (1992), an NCAA Men's Basketball Final Four (1992), and a World Series (1987 and 1991).

25) Killebrew Drive.

26) 537 (yes, only 537, and it came in their pennant-winning year of 1965, on Sept. 20)

27) The center-field flag-pole. For many years, it served as the flag-pole at the Richfield American Legion Post.

28) April 6 (Milwaukee beats Minnesota 7-2 in 53 degree temps)

29) 1988. The Twins, of course, were defending world champions. In 1992, a year after their second world title, they drew an average of 30,647. Teams usually draw their largest attendance the year following a World Series title.

30) Yes. During three seasons, the Twins have drawn under 10,000 per game: 1981 (7,951), 1974 (8,603), and 1976 (9,539).

31) 39,504.

32) Two layers of teflon-coated fiberglass.

33) 53 degrees

34) 89 degrees. By the way, it was not the latest date for an opener, as April 23, 1972 was, but it was 44 degrees and rainy that year.

35) 23 feet, the exact same as at the Metrodome.

36) Four hours

37) "The Homerdome," a misnomer. In reality, it became more difficult to hit a homer in it than the major-league average over the next 25 years.

38) Kirby Puckett's Memorial Service

39) HOK Sport of Kansas City, the same firm that designed Xcel Energy Center in St. Paul and ballparks such as Camden Yards. The local architect was HGA Architects and the primary construction company was Mortenson Construction.

40) The Beatles. John, Ringo, Paul, and George played. It was a Saturday night and the English rock-stars played for about 35 minutes after four previous acts. Concert tickets cost $5.50 and $7.50.No photographers or fans were allowed on the field. The group played on a small stage near second base. No word on how many errors they made!

41). Via helicopter. Kaat lived in Eagan and the Cedar Avenue Bridge across the Minnesota River was impassable because of snow and ice.

16

INFAMOUS HAPPENINGS, IGNOMINIOUS PLAYS, UNUSUAL INCIDENTS

1) What Twins pitcher holds the major-league record for most career losses without a win?

2) In 1969, manager Billy Martin punched out starting pitcher Dave Boswell outside what Detroit bar?

3) Which Twins pitcher hurled a 5-inning perfect game on Aug. 6, 1967, at Met Stadium?

4) What player, on Sept. 5, 1978, strutted slowly toward home plate from third base and then took several steps backward and missed it, only touching the plate after another runner had crossed it? (He was called out, by the way.)

5) How many times was Harmon Killebrew awarded with a sacrifice in his 8,018 plate appearances with the Twins?

6) What Twins batter has the most-consecutive at-bats without a hit? (Yes, it is a pitcher.)

7) What Twins player used a bat to smash manager Ron Gardenhire's office door during the 2007 season, (his last as a Twin)?

8) Enterprising fans and youth were able to enter games at Met Stadium without paying the stipend for a ticket by: A) Walking in hand-in-hand with owner Calvin Griffith; B) Squeezing through a small hole in a fence rimming the perimeter of the stadium; C) Slipping an usher a bottle of Hamm's beer; D) Stealing your brother's ushering outfit and claiming you were late and needed to get to your station as soon as possible.

9) What was odd about the 3-game series the Twins played at California July 21-23, 1967?

10) What former Twins outfielder, then playing for the California Angels, was shot and killed in Gary, Indiana, in 1978 in a tragic case of mistaken identity?

11) When right-handed knuckleballer Joe Niekro was removed from a game on Aug. 3, 1987 in Anaheim, when it was determined he was guilty of possessing objects that could alter a baseball, who was the umpire who tossed him out of the game?

12) When Oakland's Dave "King-Kong" Kingman lofted a fly ball that entered a drainage hole in the Metrodome teflon ceiling/roof that didn't come down, what was the ruling made on the field?

13) The first game ever to be postponed at the Metrodome occurred on April 14, 1983, when the Twins were to host the California Angels. What caused the postponement?

14) Why did over 50,000 people crowd into the Metrodome on the night of Oct. 12, 1987, when a game wasn't even held their that day (it was 13 days before the game-clinching win over St. Louis in the World Series)?

15) When the Twins hosted Game 1 of the 1965 World Series, why didn't the Dodgers' top starter (Sandy Koufax) pitch for the visitors?

16) To indicate whether or not the Twins had won the previous day's ballgame, what indicator/symbol did the *Minneapolis Tribune* put on the front page of the newspaper to let readers know the result?

17) What Twins player, on four occasions, had the only Twins hit in a one-hit performance against Minnesota?

18) What two pitchers hurled perfect games against the Twins 30 years apart?

19) When a power outage in Minneapolis caused the air-conditioning to shut down at the Metrodome on August 5, 2001, how hot did the temperature get inside the building?

20) What is the poorest record, in wins, by the Twins in any month in their 48-year history?

21) What Twins fielder caught two consecutive pop-ups off the bat of Milwaukee's Rob Deer on May 30, 1992, that had ricocheted off the Metrodome ceiling?

22) For what reason did the Twins and Cleveland have to suspend their game after 11 innings on Oct. 2, 2004?

23) While under a 10 day suspension for possessing objects that could alter a baseball, Joe Niekro appeared on *Late Night With David Letterman* in New York City. What "props" did he appear on stage with?

24) In 1997, a businessman signed an agreement-in-principle that would have moved the Twins to North Carolina? What was his name?

25) Calvin Griffith gave a speech after the 1978 season in which he insulted blacks, leading Rod Carew to demand a trade? In what city and for what organization was Griffith speaking?

26) In the midst of so-called "contraction" talks with major-league baseball after the World Series in 2001, what team and owner offered to have his team contracted?

27) In the early 1980s, owner Calvin Griffith signed a 30-year contract with the Metropolitan Sports Commission which stated that the club had to draw an average of 1.4 million fans in any three-year period or he could break the lease and move the team. To what city was Calvin threatening a move?

28) On May 2, 2001 (Dollar Dog Night), unruly behavior by fans in the left-field stands interrupted a game with the Yanks' for 12 minutes after they pelted what Yankee leftfielder with hot dogs and other sundry items?

29) On Aug. 25, 1970, what prompted some of the 17,967 fans attending the Minnesota-Boston game at Met Stadium to mingle on the outfield grass after the game started?

30) On Sept. 22, 1968, what Twins player became just the second player in major-league history to play all nine positions in one game? In an amazing twist, who was the first batter he faced as a pitcher?

31) What was highly unusual and ironic about Harmon Killebrew's final American League home-run, which came on Sept. 18, 1975?

32) What former Twins shortstop died at age 29 at the Mayo Clinic in Rochester just six months after being traded to Texas in the Bert Blyleven trade in 1976?

33) In its final few seasons, what were the ground rules at the Metrodome regarding the ceiling and the speakers?

34) Which prolific Twins player, who spent most of his childhood in the United States, never played high school baseball?

◀ *Answers to Chapter 16* ▶

1) Terry Felton. The Twin righthander was 0-16 for his career; this included an 0-13 record in 1982, also a major-league record for most losses without a win in a season. Incidentally, he was winless in 13 decisions despite having an ERA below 5.00 and allowing less than a hit per inning pitched.

2) Lindell Athletic Club. After some arguing in the bar, some members of the team ventured to the parking lot outside the club where Boswell knocked down outfielder Bob Allison, who suffered a black eye and also injured some teeth which required dental work. Upon hearing about the incident, Martin walked out and laid into Boswell, who needed 20 stitches in the head, while Billy collected seven stitches on a knuckle. Boswell went 8-3 in 12 starts after the fight and ended up winning 20 games for the club that year. He has been adamant in stating that Martin was the best manager he ever played for.

3) Dean Chance. He retired all 15 Red Sox batters in a 2-0 Minnesota victory. After Chance struck out leading off the bottom of the 5th inning, the game was delayed and later called on account of rain. (Major-league baseball no longer considers such games officially "perfect.")

4) Danny Ford.

5) Zero. Why bunt when you hit a homer every 14 at-bats?

6) Dean Chance. Chance went 53 at-bats between hits from 1967-69. Twins players considered Chance foul balls as hits!

7) Kyle Lohse

8) You might have done the others but the only one I witnessed was B.

9) For the only time in their history, the Twins lost all three games in a series by the same score (2-1).

10) Lyman Bostock. After playing a day game against the White Sox in Chicago, Bostock was visiting relatives in Gary. He and friends were giving a woman a ride and the woman's estranged husband pulled up alongside the vehicle and shot Bostock in the head.

11) Tim Tschida. Tschida is a St. Paul native and has been a major league umpire since 1986. Nickro was found to have an emery board and a piece of sandpaper in his pocket and was suspended for 10 games.

12) Ground-rule double. This occurred on May 4, 1984.

13) A heavy snowfall on April 13 dropped more than a foot of snow on the Twin Cities and the Angels were unable to land at the airport and were diverted to Chicago. The next day a chunk of ice tore a hole in the roof, causing it to deflate, but the roof was quickly repaired and re-inflated, and the Twins and Angels played the next night. (A game was also postponed in August 2007 a day after the nearby interstate bridge across the Mississippi collapsed.)

14) The impromptu gathering took place a few hours after the Twins had defeated the Tigers in Detroit in the A.L. playoffs and it was a welcome-home celebration for the Twins team.

15) Koufax, a Jew, refused to pitch on Yom Kippur, the holiest day in the Jewish calendar. Don Drysdale pitched instead and lost 8-2 to the Twins.

16) At the top of the front page, there was a symbol of two Twins players, either smiling and shaking hands (win) or sobbing (loss).

17) Cesar Tovar

18) Catfish Hunter for Oakland (May 8, 1968) and David Wells for the New York Yankees (May 17, 1998)

19) 91 degrees.

20) 3-26 in May, 1982. The second month of that season, the first in the Metrodome, was the worst in the majors since the Philadelphia Athletics went 2-28 in June of 1916. Thus, it was the worst month by a team in 66 years.

Cesar Tovar

21) Shortstop Greg Gagne

22) Curfew. The Gopher football team was slated to play that night. The curfew simply didn't allow the Twins to start an inning after a specified time. The Twins traditionally played morning games when the University of Minnesota played games at the field later on that date in order to allow the grounds-crew to make the transition to a football configuration from the baseball one.

23) Niekro, wearing a workman's belt, had a power sander, a nail file, a clothes brush, toenail and fingernail clippers, sandpaper, tweezers, scissors, emery boards, Vaseline, and two bottles of Kiwi Scuff Magic.

24) Donald Beaver

25) Waseca (Lion's Club)

26) Minnesota Twins. Owner Carl Pohlad, allegedly told Commissioner and pal Bud Selig that the Twins would consider such action if it was deemed necessary.

27) Tampa/St. Petersburg, Florida. A group of civic leaders, led by Harvey Mackay, purchased tickets to keep the team in the Twin Cities. From mid-May to mid-June, 1984, they set up a ticket buyout that prevented the Twins from exercising the agreement.

28) Chuck Knoblauch. Forty fans were ejected from the game. Twins manager Tom Kelly helped quell the disturbance as the fans derided the former Twins star.

29) An announcement by public-address announcer Bob Casey stated that a telephone warning had been received from the Bloomington Police Dept. that an explosion would take place at the stadium. The pronouncement led to a 43-minute delay in the 4th inning. Most of the fans went to the parking lot during the delay. Tony Conigliaro later won the game 1-0 with a solo homer.

30) Cesar Tovar. And the first batter he faced was shortstop Bert Campaneris, who had been the first player to accomplish the feat on Sept. 8, 1965, against California. But Campaneris was forced to leave the game that in the 9th inning after a collision at home plate. Thus Tovar was the first to play all nine positions and play the entire game. The Twins won that day 2-1.

31) Killebrew's 573rd homer occurred at Metropolitan Stadium, where he tormented opposing pitchers for 14 years. The final round-tripper came against Twins lefthander Eddie Bane as Harmon was playing his final season with the Kansas City Royals. Killebrew, to this day, holds the A.L. record for the most homers by a right-handed batter.

32) Danny Thompson. The Kansas native died of leukemia. He had played in 694 games in seven seasons with the Twins, primarily as a shortstop.

33) A ball hitting the ceiling or speakers in fair territory that was caught by a fielder was considered an out and the runners advance at their own risk. A ball hitting the ceiling or speakers in foul territory was considered a dead ball.

34) Rod Carew. Rod played sandlot ball in New York City before being signed by scout Herb Stein.

17

TRADES AND ACQUISITIONS

1) Rightfielder Tom Brunansky, a mainstay on the 1987 Twins' world-championship club, was traded on April 22, 1988, for what Cardinals infielder?

2) When Bert Blyleven was traded to Texas in 1976 along with shortstop Danny Thompson and $250,000, what players did the Twins get in return from the Rangers?

3) Who did Minnesota trade to the Texas Rangers in exchange for pitchers Mike Smithson and John Butcher and minor-league catcher Sam Sorce before the 1984 season?

4) After the 1967 season, shortstop Zoilo Versalles and pitcher Jim "Mudcat" Grant were shipped to the Los Angeles Dodgers in return for two pitchers and a catcher. Who were they?

5) What young catcher was traded to Milwaukee on July 7, 1971, for catcher Phil Roof?

6) Prior to the 2008 season, Johan Santana was traded to the New York Mets for three pitchers and an outfielder. Who were they?

7) In another deal following the 2007 season, the Twins dealt starting shortstop Jason Bartlett, minor-leaguer Eduado Morlan, and what former #1 draft choice to Tampa Bay for outfielder Delmon Young, infielder Brendan Harris, and outfielder Jason Pridie?

8) When slick-fielding first-baseman Vic Power and pitcher Dick Stigman joined the Twins prior to the 1962 season, who did the Twins give up to procure them?

9) In perhaps the team's best trade ever, the Twins sent catcher A.J. Pierzynski and cash to the Giants in return for what pitchers in late 2003?

10) In their first trade after moving to Minnesota, which reliever did the Twins give up (along with infielder Reno Bertoia) for Kansas City outfielder Bill Tuttle?

11) When the Twins reacquired Bert Blyleven from Cleveland on August 1, 1985, what four players did they ship to the Indians in return?

12) When 1988 A.L. Cy Young winner Frank Viola was traded by the Twins on July 31, 1989, to the Mets, who were the five pitchers the Twins received in return who would help the team win the World Series two years later?

13) When Bernie Allen was traded to Washington on Dec. 3, 1966, for reliever Ron Kline, what right-handed starter was also sent to the Senators?

14) In May of 1982, what battery did the Twins send to the Yankees in exchange for pitchers Peter Filson and John Pacella and infielder Larry Milbourne?

15) A month before the above-mentioned trade (April 10, 1982) the Yanks and Twins were involved in another deal, with the Twins picking up pitchers Ron Davis and Paul Boris, and minor-league shortstop Greg Gagne, for pitcher Gary Serum and an infielder who had been a starter for more than five seasons. Who was he?

16) On Dec. 3, 2003, what Twins starter was traded to Philadelphia for Carlos Silva, Nick Punto, and Bobby Korecky?

17) In one of their best in-season swaps ever, the Twins dealt outfielder Bobby Kielty for what veteran outfielder from Toronto during the All-Star break in July of 2003?

18) Most think that Johan Santana was acquired via the Rule 5 draft, but in fact he was swapped in a Dec. 13, 1999 deal for pitcher Jared Camp. What was the other team involved in the trade?

19) All-Star Chuck Knoblauch was traded to the Yankees prior to spring training in 1998 in an arrangement that sent four players to Minnesota, including what starting pitcher?

20) In Dec. 1966, the Twins traded outfielder Jimmie Hall to the California Angels, along with first-baseman Don Mincher and pitcher Pete Cimino, for what former Cy Young award winner?

21) On Sept. 9, 2000, the Twins traded reliever Hector Carrasco to Boston for what minor league outfielder who would go on to become a fan favorite?

22) What legendary Twins star was traded for fellows named Landreaux, Engle, Havens, and Hartzell?

23) Who did the San Francisco Giants trade to the Twins just a week before the 1987 season for a player to be named later and Ray Velasquez?

24) Who did the Twins trade to the Yankees to acquire seasoned knuckleballer Joe Niekro in mid-season 1987.

25) What Yankees lefthander, who had already played 24 years in the majors, was dealt to the Twins on Aug, 31, 2003, for

Joe Nathan

pitcher Juan Padilla? (Incidentally, this same player had been traded to the New York Mets prior to the 1979 season for Minnesota-native Jerry Koosman.)

26) On April 4, 1990, the Twins traded which minor-league pitcher in order to pick up catcher Junior Ortiz and pitcher Orlando Lind from Pittsburgh?

27) What right-handed reliever was traded to the Chicago Cubs in August of 1986 for relievers George Frazier and Ray Fontenot and minor-league prospect Julius McDougal?

28) What Twins starter, who would become a future 20-game

winner for the team, was obtained from Cleveland during mid-season 1964 in return for pitcher Lee Stange and infielder George Banks?

29) What Twins hurler was traded (along with Kevin Trudeau) to California in November 1988 for Paul Sorrento, Mike Cook, and minor-league pitcher Rob Wassenaar, an Edina native?

30) On Dec. 5, 2005, the Twins got second-baseman Alexi Casilla from the Los Angeles Angels in exchange for which reliever? (Hint: he was in the bullpen for the 2008 World Champion Philadelphia Phillies.)

31) A Twins reserve catcher was traded in 1972 to the New York Yankees for Danny Walton after playing in just 41 games over four seasons. He went on to play a total of 24 seasons? Who was he?

32) What Cincinnati Reds shortstop was traded to Minnesota in November of 1968 for left-handed starter Jim Merritt?

33) What long-time Twin Cities' journalist was once traded to the Washington Senators (along with pitcher Joe Grzenda) for out-fielder Brant Alyea, who was the team's starting leftfielder in 1970 and 1971?

34) Starting pitcher Kevin Tapani and reliever Mark Guthrie were traded on July 31, 1995, to the Dodgers in return for four players, one of whom was an infielder who later earned an All-Star berth and now does baseball commentary on Fox Sports North. Who was he?

35) With what other major-league team have the Twins made the most trades?

36) On November 6, 2009, Minnesota made a trade for Milwaukee's starting shortstop, J. J. Hardy, in a straight one-for-one trade as the Twins sent the Brewers' what exciting but enigmatic and erratic outfielder?

1) Second-baseman Tommy Herr

2) Third-baseman Mike Cubbage, shortstop Roy Smalley, pitcher Bill Singer, and pitcher Jim Gideon.

3) Gary Ward

4) Relief pitchers Ron Perranoski and Bob Miller and catcher John Roseboro.

5) Paul Ratliff

6) Outfielder Carlos Gomez and pitchers Philip Humber, Kevin Mulvey, and Deolis Guerra.

7) Matt Garza

8) Pedro Ramos.

9) Joe Nathan, Francisco Liriano, and Boof Bonser

10) Paul Giel

11) Jay Bell, Jim Weaver, Curt Wardle, and Richard Yett

12) Rick Aguilera, Tim Drummond, Jack Savage, Kevin Tapani, and David West

13) Camilo Pascual

14) Roger Erickson and Butch Wynegar

15) Roy Smalley

16) Eric Milton

17) Shannon Stewart. Minnesota also acquired pitcher Dave Gassner.

18) Florida. The Twins also send the Marlins' cash in the deal.

19) Eric Milton. The Twins also got shortstop Cristian Guzman, outfielder Brian Buchanan, and minor-league pitcher Danny Mota.

20) Dean Chance. Shortstop Jackie Hernandez was also sent to Minnesota.

21) Lew Ford (2003-2007). Ford was a regular outfielder in 2004 and 2005.

22) Rod Carew. Rodney was traded to California on Feb. 3, 1979.

23) The Twins received outfielder Dan Gladden and minor-league pitcher David Blakely with Bemidji native pitcher Bryan

Hickerson being sent to the Giants on June 15 of '87 to complete the trade.

24) Catcher Mark Salas

25) Jesse Orosco. The left-handed reliever pitched in just eight games at the end of the 2003 season. Orosco was 87-80 and had a 3.16 ERA in a career that started in 1979, pitching in a total of 1,252 games, which is still the major league record.

26) Mike Pomeranz, who is now the lead anchor on KARE-11.

27) Ron Davis. The Cubs also got minor-league pitcher Dewayne Coleman.

28) Jim "Mudcat" Grant

29) Bert Blyleven

30) J.C. Romero

31) Rick Dempsey. After being drafted in 1967 by the Twins, Dempsey was traded to the Yankees and later played 11 years with the Baltimore, where he won the 1983 World Series Most Valuable Player award. He played 11 years for the Orioles and for eight teams total.

32) Leo Cardenas

33) Charley Walters. "Shooter", so nicknamed by Twins outfielder Bob Allison, was signed out of a tryout camp at Met Stadium in the summer of 1965. A lanky righthander who pitched for Minneapolis Edison, Walters is one of only three players to make it to the big leagues with the Twins after being signed out of a tryout camp. The others were Jerry Terrell (Waseca) and Gary Serum (Alexandria).

34) Ron Coomer. The happy-go-lucky Coomer was an All-Star in 1999; the others in the trade were pitchers Jose Parra and Greg Hansell, and outfielder Chris Latham, all who had brief careers with the Twins.

35) The Cleveland Indians, with 13 trades, followed by Boston (11), the Cubs (10) and the Yankees (10).

36) Carlos Gomez

Harmon Killebrew

18

TOP TWINS PLAYERS BY POSITION

FIRST BASE

1) Kent Hrbek (1981-94)

Kent enjoyed playing his first few major league games in his hometown of Bloomington at Metropolitan Stadium, though the next year the Twins moved downtown to the Metrodome. If Puckett was the heart of the team during its two World Championship seasons, and Gaetti was the soul, then Hrbek was the spine. A truly splendid fielder and a clutch hitter, he was a true clean-up hitter with power and had a great eye at the plate. His 293 homers are second among Twins sluggers behind Killebrew, and he is also second to Harmon in RBIs (1,086). Kent ranks second in walks (838), third in doubles (312), and fourth in hits (1,749), total bases (2,976), and runs (903). His first few years were his best; injuries and added bulk cut his career short. Still, he was a very fine player who cared more about team goals than individual stats. Of course, many of you were looking for Killebrew in this spot but his place is elsewhere on the diamond. Harmon played in more than 100 games at first base in only three seasons.

2) Justin Morneau (2003-)

If he remains healthy and productive, Morneau will soon surpass many of Hrbek's totals. He won the league MVP award in 2006, and might have won another in 2008 had the final two weeks in September not been so disastrous. He is one of the best long-ball and RBI threats in the American League, and might well remain a 30-homer, 100 RBI man for the next decade. Morneau is currently tied for eighth all-time among Twins in homers (163) and ranks ninth in RBI (623). His defense has improved so dramatically that he is now considered one of the top fielding first-basemen in the majors. The Canadian relishes pressure situations and is a gamer; let's hope he is still hitting his homers at Target Field when he is 35. A prediction: Statues of Justin and his pal Joe Mauer will be built on Target Plaza after both are inducted into Baseball's Hall of Fame in 2028.

3) Don Mincher (1961-66)

In his six seasons, Mincher knocked out 90 homers and was a threat to pitchers if they were able to get by studs like Oliva and Killebrew. Not acrobatic at first, he was merely serviceable in the field. People tend to forget what a force he could be as a tough left-handed hitter. He is currently tied for sixth among Twins in slugging percentage (.479).

4) Paul Molitor (1996-98)

Though "Molly" played just three seasons with his childhood team at the end of his Hall of Fame career, those years were superlative. Used mostly as a designated hitter, in 1996 he led the league with 225 hits (at the age of 40!) and hit an astounding .341 with 113 RBI. He batted .312 over those three seasons, knocked in 273 runs, scored 247 runs, and totaled 103 doubles. He continued to be one of the game's most dynamic baserunners at age 42. We knew he was good but until we saw him play every day, we had no idea he was that savvy and smart. He was truly one of the best all-round players of the last quarter of the 20th century.

SECOND BASE

1) Rod Carew (1967-78)

Sir Rodney won all seven of his A.L. batting titles with the Twins (1969, 1972-75, 1977-78) and was the top bunter of his era. A true artist with the bat and an expert baserunner (271 steals) he stands alongside Tony Gwynn and Wade Boggs as one of the three top hitters for average in the past 40 years. He averaged .334 as a Twin (still the record) and was a perennial All-Star for the team. He played nine years at second before switching to first base in 1976. He reached his peak of productivity in 1977 with career highs in homers (14),

RBIs (100), hits (239), runs (128), doubles (38), and triples (16)—a magical year that earned him the league Most Valuable Player award. Carew is tops among Twins in triples (90), second in hits (2,085) and stolen bases (271), third in runs (950), fourth in doubles (305) and walks (613), and fifth in total bases (2,792). He was a maestro with the bat, flicking the ball around with the artistry of an orchestra conductor.

2) Chuck Knoblauch (1991-97)

"Knobby" took over the leadoff role in 1991 and played like a 10-year vet as a rookie. He was a great contact hitter and a superb base-stealer. On defense, he was quick and scrappy, the "Dan Gladden" of the '91 World Series champs. Knoblauch stole 276 bases, an all-time Twins high, and scored at least 100 runs four times. The intense infielder hit .304 during his Twins' career and ranks third in on-base percentage (.391), fifth in triples (51), sixth in runs (713), and eighth in hits (1,197). He could help the team win a game in as many ways as any player in Twins' history.

3) Rob Wilfong (1977-82)

While he was only a regular for four seasons, the slender Californian had range and speed and witnessed enough of Carew to become a great bunter. He even hit .313 in 1979. Rob is one of those guys who gets overlooked. Gene Mauch liked him a lot, that's good enough for me.

4) Steve Lombardozzi (1985-88)

With "Lombo" in this spot, it is apparent that this is the weakest position in Twins' history. Lombardozzi was a solid defender and turned the double play well and was a standout in the '87 Series (hitting .412). Tim Teufel was a possibility here with three good seasons but his defensive liabilities cancel out his hitting acumen. Bernie Allen (1961-64) had a good rookie year and than faded. Two more healthy years from Castino after making the switch from third would have put him here.

SHORTSTOP

1) Zoilo Versalles (1961-67)

Except for his electrifying MVP year in 1965, when he lead the league in six categories, Zoilo's statistics aren't all that impressive. In '65, he was sensational, tops in the A.L. in runs (126), doubles (45), triples (12), total bases (308), at-bats (666), and plate appearances (728). Zoilo did lead the league in triples three years and his power at the plate was a bit unusual for shortstops of that era. He was a spectacular playmaker in the field but was also error-prone, especially on routine plays. Versalles still ranks tied for 10th in hits (1,046) and 10th in total bases (1,604). Zoilo was a lot more flash than substance but for four years, he was as talented and as exciting a shortstop as existed in the big leagues.

2) Greg Gagne (1983-92)

Greg Gagne

"Gags" only hit .249 during his Twins career and never did quite learn how to steal bases despite his great speed (fewer than 10 per season) but he was unquestionably the best defensive shortstop in the Twins' 48-year history. He had great range and really solidified the defense up the middle. Watching him go from first to third on a single to the outfield was a true joy. He is a classic case of defensive exploits more than making up for offensive deficiencies. Combine this with Gagne's durability and he may be one of the most under-rated Twins' players.

3) Roy Smalley (1976-82; 1985-87)

"Roy Boy" wasn't just the nephew of Twin manager Gene Mauch; he could play. Stylish as a fielder yet lacking great range, he had some pop at the plate, as evidenced by his 108 homers as a Twin—and he had a good knowledge of the strike zone. When he returned to the club in 1985 he was a leader and an effective platoon player and pinch-hitter. Smalley is 10th all-time in RBI (485), at-bats (3,997), and games played (1,148) and tied for 10th in hits (1,046). Was Roy the most erudite or articulate fellow to ever play for the Twins? Maybe!

4) Leo Cardenas (1969-71)

Cardenas was a solid player for three seasons, playing first under Billy Martin's tutelage and then for Bill Rigney. He had 83 doubles and 39 homers in just three seasons and nary missed a game. Somewhat overshadowed in Twins history, Cardenas was one of the top overall shortstops in the game for his three years here. Adept around the bag, the Twins' double-play capability was first-rate with him in the midst of it.

THIRD BASE

1) Harmon Killebrew (1961-74)

Though he played more games at first (872) than third (508), the "Killer" fills out our team best at this spot. He won his MVP award in 1969 playing mostly at third base. Harm had decent reactions at third and did have a good arm. Of course, his career was mostly about hitting and he knocked out 475 homers as a Twin. One of the top home-run hitters in history, he was 5th in career home runs until the steroid era changed all that. Killebrew remains the top right-handed home-run hitter in A.L. history and is in the top five in home-run frequency, hitting a round-tripper every 14.28 times at bat. Harmon was one of the most feared hitters of his or any generation, and played over 100 games a year nine times at three different positions (third base, first base, and left field). The only thing as prodigious as his homeruns was his well-deserved reputation as a gentleman.

2) Gary Gaetti (1981-90)

The "Rat" was a bulwark at third, showing no fear on line-shots coming his way and then winging the ball with that powerful arm. Gaetti's determination and guts were a key to the rise of the Twins' in the mid-1980's. He was one of the four of five best in the game at the hot corner. He's sixth all-time among Twins in homers (201), hitting at least 20 homers on six different occasions, and ranks among the top ten in several other offensive categories. Gary is sixth in RBI (758), total bases (2,181), doubles (252), hits (1,276), games played (1,361), and at-bats (4,989) Durable and tough, his value went way beyond his stats. Inducted into the Twins' Hall of Fame in 2007, Gaetti was the opening day third-baseman nine straight years. He has the best fielding percentage of any Twins third-baseman (.977).

3) Rich Rollins (1961-1968)

The stocky third-sacker was a mainstay for the Twins in the early years in Bloomington. He hit 71 homers and had 369 RBI in six years as a starter. Solid but not flashy, he was acceptable in the field and a reliable right-handed hitter, batting sixth or seventh in a power-laden lineup that was probably the strongest in the majors during that time.

4) Corey Koskie (1998-2004)

The Canadian was a vital part in the Twins' resurgence over the past decade. Koskie made himself into a fine defensive third-baseman and a strong left-handed hitter at the plate with a lot of hard work. Corey was a tough out, a good baserunner, and a character. Koskie gets the nod here over John Castino, whose injuries cut short a promising career.

CATCHER

1) Joe Mauer (2004 -   )

Being the top draft pick in 2001, and bearing the burden of being the "hometown kid," has not prevented Mauer from becoming the team's top career catcher and one of the game's current superstars. Joe's on-base percentage and average with runners in scoring position has been among the best in the majors since his arrival in the big leagues. His eye at the plate is incredible and he is a very astute baserunner. He has already won three batting titles (.347 in '06, .328 in '08, and .365 in '09) and should challenge for a few more. Concerns about his lack of power were dispelled in 2009, a stellar season during which he led the league in slugging percentage and was a near-unanimous selection for the league's MVP award. On top of accomplishments as one of the best-hitting catchers in major-league history, Joe has won Gold Glove awards the past two seasons. The question is, could he possibly get even better?

2) Earl Battey (1961-67)

Battey was a large man who could drive the ball and hit when it counted. His average stood above .280 for four seasons, which is impressive for such a slow-footed runner. Earl made five All-Star teams and hit 76 homers in his seven-year career as a Twin. Also highly skilled behind the plate, Earl possessed a fine throwing arm, often picking off runners, and he was as steady as can be on a pop foul. Battey was one of the top catchers in the game for several seasons and was a classy man as well.

3) Brian Harper (1988-93)

Harper was never considered a good handler of pitchers; nor did he possess a strong arm. Harper's forte was hitting, where he ranks sixth among Twins in average (.306) and was considered one of the league's toughest outs during his tenure here. Brian hit over .300 four times and never hit under .294. He was a great two-strike hitter; he struck out only once for every 20 at-bats. In the '91 World Series, he made several sparkling plays at the plate. Witnessing a Harper at-bat was a treat, a right-handed version of A.J. Pierzynski fouling off nasty pitches.

4) Butch Wynegar (1976-1982)

Butch started in the majors as a 20-year-old in 1976 and became a fan favorite, though he never really reached the "star" potential that was predicted for him. Wynegar was durable and a solid backstop with accomplished defensive skills even as a youngster. Butch hit .260 and .261 his first two years and hit 10 homers both years with 69 and 79 RBI's those first two seasons. Calvin "really liked that kid" but still traded him to the Yankees in the middle of his sixth season with the Twins.

LEFT FIELD

1) Bob Allison (1961-70)

The former Kansas football star hit 211 homers in his 10-year career here. A big guy, he was a good baserunner and a capable fielder. He's still third among Twins in homers and eighth in RBIs (796), runs (648), total bases (1,881) and triples (41). Bob brought his football mentality to the diamond and though strikeout-prone, helped his buddy Harmon see better pitches. Formed a formidable lineup with Oliva, Killebrew, Mincher, et al. in the 1960's.

2) Cesar Tovar (1965-72)

They called him "Pepe" and that described his all-out swashbuckling style. He could play all positions and became the second person in history to actually do so in 1968 against Oakland. Cesar was an energetic leadoff man and was an aggressive runner. Cesar is third (186) in stolen bases, seventh in triples (45), ninth in hits (1,164) and doubles (193), and is tied for ninth in runs (646). He played equally in the outfield and infield and is probably the most versatile Twins' player ever, along with Denny Hocking. He's Punto with more ability at the plate. Cesar once led the A.L. in doubles and triples in 1970.

3) Dan Gladden (1987-91)

When Gladden came over from the Giants during spring training of 1987, he became their leadoff man and a sure-handed outfielder who caught anything his swift strides could get him to. Though he didn't walk much, his dogged demeanor gave his new team the edge it needed after finishing last the previous year. He stole 116 bases in his six years and was fearless in whatever he did. Danny judged flyballs perhaps better than any Twins outfielder besides Puckett. Gladden's "no-holes-barred" style was a key ingredient in two World Series title drives.

4) Larry Hisle (1973-77)

Hisle was a class act who came from the Phillies and gave the team a standout, all-around ballplayer. He hit over .300 twice and totaled 87 homers in his five seasons; in 1977 he led the league with 119 RBIs. Larry possessed good speed which allowed him to cut off balls in the gap and run the bases with aplomb; however, an arm injury allowed runners to take risks on the bases. In 1976 he had 31 stolen bases and 16 outfield assists.

CENTER FIELD

1) Kirby Puckett (1984-95)

Kirby was the face of the franchise for 12 seasons and with good reason. He hit .318 during his shortened career and won six Gold Gloves. He was noted for his homer-saving catches but his arm was also strong and accurate. Did he ever miss a cut-off man? Kirby was an intuitive fielder, rarely leaving his feet and rarely getting fooled on a ball hit his way. Puckett is tops on the all-time Twins' chart in hits (2,304), total bases (3,453), doubles (414), and is second in runs scored (1,071) and games played (1,783). He's third in RBIs (1,085) and triples (57), fourth in stolen bases (134), and fifth in homers (207). One can only imagine the stats he would have put up if not for his career-ending eye injury. Only one player had more hits in his first 10 seasons as a major-leaguer. Kirby hit the ball more squarely than anyone in Twins history. Matters of athletic ability aside, Kirby was arguably the most beloved Twins player of all time. A true crowd-pleaser, he was a baseball mete-orite that all of baseball enjoyed. How lucky we were to get to watch the "Magnificent Cube"?

2) Torii Hunter (1997- 2007)

The identity of the Twins (along with Johan Santana) in the first decade of the new millenium, Hunter brimmed with confidence once he got comfortable at the plate. He hit 192 homers with the Twins (at least 25 in five seasons) but didn't learn to hit in the clutch until his final two seasons. Torii is in the top eight in several Twins hitting categories: RBI, hits, total bases, runs, and doubles. He's also fifth in steals (126). In his prime, he was considered the best centerfielder in the major leagues and his highlight-reel catches and extremely accurate arm allowed Twins hurlers to pitch with greater confidence. He was probably the best fielding outfielder in Twins history, and he was still getting better in his early 30's when he left for Los Angeles.

3) Jimmie Hall (1963-66)

Hall hit 33 homers in his rookie year, but the promising slugger faded early, hitting 20 and 25 round-trippers over the next two years before slumping to 7 in 1966 before being traded to California. A beaning in Baltimore may have made him gun-shy at the plate, and his career ended in 1970, but he was a star for the Twins in the 1960's heyday.

4) Lyman Bostock (1975-77)

Immensely talented, Bostock's smooth stroke from the left side made him a rising star. He had a breakout year in '77, when the Twins offense roared and he hit .336, a year after hitting .323, and he was developing power, too. Though overshadowed by Carew, Lyman was improving in the field and might have won a batting title with his new team, the Angels, but a senseless murder took his life in 1977.

RIGHT FIELD

1) Tony Oliva (1962-76)

"Tony O" was arguably the best pure hitter in Twins history. He might well have been the A.L's best overall hitter between 1964 and 1971, when a knee injury cost him sure-fire entry into Cooperstown. Oliva sprayed the ball to all fields, and led the league in hitting three times, in doubles four times, and in hits five times. After a poor start in the field, he became a solid outfielder. Despite his injuries, he's still second in team history in doubles (329), third in hits (1,917), total bases (3,002) and homers (220) and fourth in RBIs (947). Tony is tied for 7th among Twins in lifetime batting average at .304. If arthroscopic knee surgery would have come along a few years earlier, Oliva would have put even more remarkable numbers. The fans still adore him and his signature smile is still readily flashed.

2) Tom Brunansky (1982-1988)

Bruno, picked up in a trade with California, smacked 163 homers in his six full seasons as a strong-armed rightfielder. Brunansky never hit for much of an average but was a solid hitter behind Puckett and Hrbek. Similar to Cuddyer in many respects both on and off the field, Bruno was always a threat to hit it out of the park. His trade to St. Louis for Tommy Herr backfired in '88 and the Twins regretted the move.

3) Shane Mack (1990-1994)

A skilled ballplayer and superlative athlete who was overshadowed by Puckett and friends. Does it surprise you that Shane has the fifth-highest all-time batting average as a Twin at .309, after Carew, Mauer, Molitor, and Puckett? His emergence in 1991 was a key factor in their World Series title. Mack, a rule 5 pickup from San Diego, was one of the best bargains in Twins' history.

4) Jacque Jones (1999-2005)

Amused? Don't be. We all know that Jacque never did quite learn the strike zone, like his buddy Torii, but he could hit. Jacque was a top-flight fielder playing in Hunter's shadow, and he could play all the outfield spots equally well. Jacque hit 136 homers as a Twin and batted better than .300 twice. He could steal a base, too. His overly aggressive

147

demeanor at the plate cost him a chance to be a truly special player, though he had as much raw talent as Torii.

STARTING PITCHERS: (RIGHT-HANDED)

1) Bert Blyleven (1970-76; 1985-88)

Before he became popular as the color-man on Twins TV broadcasts, Blyleven was, for two decades, one of the top starters in the majors. He ranks first in club history in shutouts (29), strikeouts (2,035) and complete games (141). Bert is second in wins (149), innings-pitched (2,566⅔), and is third in games started (345). He suffered many hard-luck losses due to lack of run support, but he was durable and his curveball was one of the best of his generation. He was effective as a 19-year old in 1970 and was a team leader during his second stint with the team when they won the World Series in 1987. He was a true character who had fun with the game but was dead serious when toe-ing the rubber on the mound. Forget the objectivity, he is the author's favorite player!

2) Jim Perry (1963-72)

He started as a reliever after his trade from Cleveland but he was a consistent and reliable starter for several years. Perry won the A.L. Cy Young award in 1970, when he won 24 games. The previous year, he went 20-6. His earned-run average was a sparkling 3.15, third-best for a starter in team history. Perry ranks fourth in both career wins (128) and shutouts (17) and is fifth in complete games (61). Perry was also a fine fielder and, like many of the top pitchers of that era for the Twins, an effective hitter.

3) Camilo Pascual (1961-66)

The Cuban-born Pascual was dynamite in his first three seasons in Minnesota, leading the league in strikeouts in all three seasons and winning 20 games in '62 and 21 in '63. Camilo had a high leg kick and a great overhand curveball, which wowed the crowds on the

Bloomington prairie in those early years. He was slowed by injuries by 1965 but still ranks in the top ten in several pitching categories, including third in shutouts (18). He is eighth, despite his relatively-short tenure with the Twins', in wins (88), games started (179), and innings-pitched (1,284-⅔).

4) Brad Radke (1995-2006)

His calm demeanor hid a fierce competitiveness on the mound. In the first half of his career with the Twins, Radke pitched for some dreadful squads but he always gave the team a chance to win by virtue of his pinpoint control and his intelligent mastery of the plate. Radke is third in wins (148) and is second to Jim Kaat in games started (377); he's third in innings-pitched (2,445) and strikeouts (1,467). Radke was professorial in his approach to the game and his guile and finesse made him the true thinking-man's pitcher.

STARTING PITCHERS (LEFT-HANDED)

1) Jim Kaat (1961-73)

The classy, crafty lefthander from Michigan was a fixture for his 12-plus seasons here and one of the league's steadiest performers. Sadly, Calvin Griffth thought he was washed up and let him go to the White Sox. He pitched for various teams for another decade. Kaat ranks first all-time among Twins in several pitching categories including wins (189), games started (422), and innings-pitched (2,959⅔) and is second in complete games (133), shutouts (23), and strikeouts (1,824). He was a stellar fielder, of course, winning 12 straight Gold Gloves as a Twin (1962-73). "Kitty" was also a decent hitter and a smart baserunner.

2) Johan Santana (2000-07)

Considering that he didn't really become a full-fledged starter until the 2004 season, this Venezuelan became one of the dominant pitchers in the majors and the face of the Twins. Johan won two Cy Young awards (2004 and 2006) and won the pitching triple crown in 2006.

He was arguably the top pitcher in baseball over a five-year period between 2003 and 2007, when he was just about unbeatable at home. His ability to blow his fastball past hitters and then get them flailing at his same-motion change-up was a treat to witness. Santana led the A.L. in strikeouts in three successive years (2004-2006). He ranks fourth among Twins in strikeouts (1,381), fourth in earned-run-average (3.22), and seventh in wins (93), while his winning percentage of .679 (93-44) is tops all-time for a Minnesota starter! All of this, mind you, in just 175 Twins starts.

3) Frank Viola (1982-89)

"Sweet Music" will forever be remembered for winning the 1987 World Series Most Valuable Player award but he was also one of the AL's top lefties in the mid-1980's. Viola could change speeds well and his emotional fire and animation helped fuel the team to great heights. Frankie ranks fifth among Twins in wins (112), strikeouts (1,214) and innings-pitched (1,772-⅔). He was the A.L. Cy Young award winner in 1988 after winning 24 games. Plus, he had one of the great laughs in Twins' annals!

4) Geoff Zahn (1977-80)

This lefthander was a key veteran on a young Twins' staff, along with Jerry Koosman for a few years. Zahn was not overpowering but started 126 games over those four seasons and won 53. Let's face it, the Twins' haven't had many strong left-handed starters, at least not for more than a few seasons. Jim Merritt (1965-68) would have been the choice here but he got traded to Cincinnati!

RELIEVERS: (RIGHT-HANDED)

1) Joe Nathan (2004-2009)

Nathan, in his six seasons for the Twins, has been as good as any closer in the game, excepting only Mariano Rivera. He has the arm, the durability, and the proper mental acuity for this critical role. Joe's value to the team cannot be understated. He has racked up 246 saves from 2004 to 2009 and his opponent batting average and strikeout-to-walk ratio is exceptional. His earned-run average, not always the most accurate depiction of a reliever's value, is the best in team history for a pitcher with at least 250 appearances at 1.87. Joe has five of the top 11 annual save totals in Twins history.

2) Rick Aguilera (1989-98)

"Aggie", now enshrined in the Twins' Hall of Fame (2008), was one of the top closers in the game in the 1990's and he still is the all-time leader among Twins in saves with 254. Rick was a key cog on the '91 World Series winner and he saved 42 and 41 games in '91 and '92. Rick is second on the all-time Minnesota list in games pitched with 490 and spent two separate stints with the team. His cool persona on the mound was a steadying influence. A nice guy and a favorite of the ladies, too, just ask my wife!

3) Jeff Reardon (1987-89)

While his statistics aren't mind-boggling, his presence on the 1987 team gave the team the confidence it needed after dealing with the late-game collapses of former closer Ron Davis. Reardon totaled 104 saves in his three years with the club, with a high of 42 in 1988. The bearded-one had the attitude that he was going to throw it right by the hitters and usually did, and that element was a huge stepping-stone for a team that had sorely lacked that commodity.

4) Al Worthington (1964-69)

The reliable and consistent Worthington was a throw-back to the days when relievers pitched as many as three innings to close out games. Al, a real gentleman, spent six years as a valuable reliever. In fact, his ERA numbers for his first five seasons were 1.37, 2.41, 2.46, 2.84, and 2.71. He had 88 saves in those seasons and led the league with 18 in '68. Worthington's ERA with the Twins' was 2.62, second only to Nathan.

Relievers: (Left-handed)

1) Ron Perranoski (1968-1971)

Perranoski, obtained from the Dodgers, was a stalwart for the Twins. He led the A.L. in saves with 31 in 1969 and 34 in 1970 with an ERA of just over 2.00 in both seasons. He also pitched in well over 100 innings both years, an indication that so-called "closers" had to go more than just a single inning to earn a save. In the early days with the new save rule, he was one of the best. Certainly, one of the top late-game relievers during that four-year span.

2) Eddie Guardado (1993-03; 2008)

While not possessing "lights-out" stuff, Eddie's best quality was his determination. Guardado also had the guts to pitch inside and move the ball around and usually kept it exciting with his high-pitch counts. Eddie began his career as a starter but settled into being a decent middle-reliever before being given the "closer" job by default. He responded with a league-leading save total of 45 in 2002 and totaled 41 more in 2003. He is first all-time for the Twins in games pitched with 648.

3) Mark Guthrie (1989-95)

Guthrie was somewhat under the radar during his Twins career but with a paucity of clear-cut candidates, here he is. Guthrie had 197 appearances as a middle reliever, perhaps the least-recognized portion of a baseball team.

4) Billy Pleis (1961-66)

"Shorty" Pleis, just 5' 10" and 170 pounds, was a solid and trusted reliever for Sam Mele's Twins in the 1960s. Pleis had a 21-16 record during that time in 180 relief appearances.

19

TWINS PLAYOFFS AND POST-SEASON

1) In the first one-game playoff in Twins history, who defeated Minnesota 1-0 to win the A.L. Central title on Sept. 30, 2008?

2) What Twins right-hander beat the Anaheim Angels 2-1 at the Metrodome in the first game of the 2002 A.L.C.S?

3) Since the Twins last won a playoff series against Oakland in 2002, what is their overall post-season record?

4) In the first-ever year for divisional playoffs in 1969, what team beat the Twins 3-0 to win the A.L. pennant before going on to lose to the New York Mets in the World Series?

5) In total, how many seasons have the Twins participated in the playoffs?

6) Who are the three teams the Twins have faced at least twice in post-season action?

7) In regard to post-season series, what is the Twins all-time record?

8) What is the Twins overall post-season game record?

9) How many total post-season games have been at Met Stadium and how many were played at the Metrodome?

10) In the 1970 American League Championship Series, what team outscored the Twins 27-10 in a three-game sweep and went on to whip the Reds in the World Series?

11) Since Minnesota's decisive win in Game 7 of the 1991 World Series, what is their post-season record?

12) In both 2003 and 2004, the Twins won the first game of the A.L. Divisional Series on the road against what foe?

13) Who hit .429 in the Twins A.L.C.S. in 1991 against Toronto?

14) Who led the Twins in the 1987 A.L.C.S. by hitting .412 with two homers and nine RBI?

15) What Tigers starter, traded for minor-league pitcher John Smoltz, lost two games in the 1987 A.L. championship series against the Twins?

16) What Toronto Blue Jays pitcher became the first opponent hurler to win a post-season game at the Metrodome in the '91 playoffs?

17) Who was the backup catcher for the Twins in 1987? (Hint: his son, Drew, also a catcher, made the Twins 2010 Opening Day roster.)

18) What Twins hurler was 2-0 against Detroit in the '87 A.L.C.S.?

19) What left-handed reliever for the Twins, acquired in the Frank Viola trade, won the game-clinching Game 5 of the 1991 A.L.C.S. against Toronto?

20) What Twins reliever, a pitching coach for the Cleveland Indians for several years, pitched 5 1/3 innings of perfect relief in the '91 A.L.C.S?

21) Who slammed a three-run homer off Juan Rincon to help the Yankees overcome a 5-1 lead and beat the Twins 6-5 to win the 2004 A.L. Division Series in 2004? (Hint: he later became the Twins designated hitter.)

22) What Twins player has the highest lifetime batting average (30 at-bats minimum) in the post-season?

23) Which Twins pitcher holds the team mark for most post-season wins with four despite playing for the team for just one season?

24) What Twins player holds the post-season record for round-trippers with five?

25) Since their arrival in Minnesota in 1961, what is the longest span between playoff appearances for the Twins?

26) What Twins reliever gave up Pat Sheridan's two-run homer in the 8th inning to give Detroit a 7-6 win in Game 3 of the 1987 A.L.C.S.?

27) In both the 1987 and 1991 American League playoffs, the Twins won the A.L. pennant in how many games?

28) In what stadiums did the Twins clinch playoff wins over Detroit (1987), Toronto (1991), and Oakland (2002)?

29) What Twins hitter had six extra-base hits (two homers and four doubles) in the 1987 A.L.C.S.?

30) Who was the only Toronto player to homer for the Blue Jays in their loss to Minnesota in the '91 American League championship?

31) Counting regular-season and playoff games, what was Minnesota's record against the world champion Yankees in 2009?

32) Trailing 1-0 in the 2009 A.L. divisional series against New York, the Twins lost 4-3 in 11 innings. How many runners did they leave stranded on the basepaths in that game?

33) What Twins player made a base-running gaffe in Game 3 of the 2009 A.L divisional series against the Yankees' at the Metrodome, which Minnesota ultimately lost 4-1?

34) After the 2009 post-season had concluded for the Twins, their losing streak in post-season home games at the Metrodome had stretched to how many games?

35) What New York Yankee slugger tied game two of the 2009 A.L. Division Series with a two-run homer off closer Joe Nathan in the bottom of the ninth at Yankee Stadium?

36) What Twins player knocked in Carlos Gomez with the winning run in the 6-5 (12 innings) win over the Tigers' in the final regular-season game at the Metrodome to determine the A.L. Central champion on Oct. 6, 2009?

1) Chicago White Sox. The teams were tied with identical 88-74 records after the regulation 162 games. The game was played at Comiskey Park in Chicago as the Sox won a coin flip, despite the Twins having a 10-8 record against them to that point. The rule was changed after the post-season and the next year the Twins hosted the tie-break game against Detroit because they won the season series against the Tigers. Jim Thome, who later signed with the Twins prior to the 2010 season, homered for the only run.

2) Joe Mays

3) 3-16. Minnesota lost to Anaheim 4-1 in 2002, lost to N.Y. 3-1 in 2003, lost to N.Y. 3-1 in 2004, lost 3-0 to Oakland in 2006 and lost to N.Y. 3-0 in 2009.

4) Baltimore Orioles

5) Ten (1965, 1969, 1970, 1987, 1991, 2002, 2003, 2004, 2006, 2009)

6) Baltimore (1969, 1970); New York (2003, 2004, 2009); and Oakland (2002, 2006)

7) Five wins and eight losses

8) 25-36

9) Seven played at Met Stadium (1965, 1969, 1970) and 23 played at the Metrodome (1987, 1991, 2002, 2003, 2004, 2006, 2009)

10) Baltimore Orioles (10-6, 11-3, 6-1)

11) 6-18; all under the tutelage of manager Ron Gardenhire.

12) New York Yankees. However, they lost both series when they lost the next three games after taking those 1-0 series leads.

13) Kirby Puckett

14) Tom Brunansky

15) Doyle Alexander

16) Juan Guzman (5-2 Toronto win in Game 2)

17) Sal Butera.

18) Bert Blyleven

19) David West

20) Carl "Big Train" Willis

21) Ruben Sierra

22) Michael Cuddyer. "Cuddy" has a .365 average (23 for 63).

23) Jack Morris. "Black Jack" won two games in the A.L. championship Series against Toronto and two more in the World Series against Atlanta in 1991. In his five games in the post-season with Minnesota, Morris had a 2.23 ERA in 36 innings.

24) Kirby Puckett. Greg Gagne is second with four.

25) 17 years. After losing to Baltimore 3-0 in the 1970 A.L. championship series, the Twins didn't play in the post-season until 1987, when they earned their first-ever world title.

26) Jeff Reardon

27) Five (4-1)

28) Detroit (Tiger Stadium); Toronto (SkyDome); Oakland (Oakland Alameda)

29) Tom Brunansky

30) Joe Carter. The righthanded slugger would later go on to be the M.V.P. of the 1993 World Series.

31) 0-10. The Yanks had beaten the Twins in all seven games during the regular season and dispatched them 3-0 in the playoff matchup.

32) 17 (yes, 17)

33) Nick Punto. The hustling infielder was the tying run in the eighth inning and was at second-base when Denard Span chopped a ball up the middle. Punto assumed the ball went through to the outfield but Derek Jeter cut it off and softly tossed it home to Jorge Posada, who relayed the ball to Alex Rodriguez for the easy tag-out at third.

34) Eight games

35) Alex Rodriguez. The ninth-inning homer set up Mark Texeira's game-winning solo homer off of Jose Mijares leading off the bottom of the 11th to give New York a 2-0 series lead.

36) Alexi Casilla

Jim Kaat

20

WORLD SERIES 1965

1) What Dodgers third-baseman made the key defensive play in Game 7 of the World Series when he stabbed Zoilo Versalles' grounder down the line with two runners on in the fifth inning?

2) What Twins batter hit a three-run homer in the third inning of Game 1 at Met Stadium to power an 8-2 Minnesota victory?

3) What weak-hitting Twins infielder, a rookie, had two hits in the third inning of Game 1?

4) What former Twins player was the club's third-base coach in the '65 Fall Classic and later went on to manage the club?

5) When Sandy Koufax shut out the Twins 2-0 to win the final game at the Met, how many hits did the Twins total?

6) What Dodgers outfielder hit the only homer in the Dodger's Game 7 victory?

7) How many Twins batters hit .300 or higher in the '65 Series?

8) How many days' rest did Sandy Koufax have before he faced the Twins in Game 7 at Metropolitan Stadium?

9) What Twins fielder made one of the great catches in World Series history when he snagged Jim Lefebvre's liner down the left-field line in the Game 2 on the wet grass at Met Stadium?

10) What Twins pitcher was paired against Sandy Koufax in three of the seven games of the '65 World Series, beating him 5-1 in Game 2?

11) What Twins pitcher won two games in the '65 World Series, copping games 1 and 6?

12) Who was the starting and losing pitcher in Game 7 of the 1965 World Series, losing 2-0 on Oct. 14 at Metropolitan Stadium?

13) What Hall of Fame hurler, who played in the 1965 Series for the Dodgers, had also been on their roster during the 1955 Series?

14) What Twins team representative doubled off Sandy Koufax in the lefthander's first game for the Brooklyn Dodgers at Ebbets Field back in 1955?

15) In Games 3 and 5 in Los Angeles, what two Dodger pitchers shut out the Twins 4-0 and 7-0, respectively?

16) During the 1965 season, what was the Twins record playing in Los Angeles?

17) What former Dodger clubhouse boy pitched two innings of relief against his hometown team in the '65 Series?

18) Who was the Most Valuable Player of the 1965 World Series?

19) Who led the Twins in RBIs in the 1965 World Series with four?

20) What two Dodgers' relievers later became relievers for the Twins?

21) What was the name of the stadium and the area of Los Angeles where the Dodgers' played their games starting in 1962?

22) What Twin hit a three-run homer in Game 6 to propel the Twins to a 5-1 win over the Dodgers, evening the World Series at three games apiece?

23) Which Dodger outfielder led his team with seven runs scored and six RBI while also hitting two homers?

24) How many strikeouts did Sandy Koufax total in his three starts against the Twins?

25) Which Dodgers' infielder, who hit .400, had a son who later broadcast Twins games on both radio and television?

26) What was the Twins batting average during the '65 Series?

27) Who did Sandy Koufax strike out to win the World Series title?

28) A team noted for its speed, which two Dodgers runners led the speedy Los Angeles club with three stolen bases?

29) Who was the only Twins batter besides Zoilo Versalles to triple for the Twins in the 1965 World Series?

30) What two Twins sluggers homered for the only runs for Minnesota in a 7-2 loss in Game 4?

31) Who composed the switch-hitting Dodgers' infield in the '65 Fall Classic?

◄ *Answers to Chapter 20* ►

1) Jim "Junior" Gilliam

2) Zoilo Versalles

3) Second-baseman Frank Quilici hit a double and a single off Don Drysdale. For the entire series he went just 4 for 20, hitting a lowly .200. During the season he had hit .208 in 56 games with just seven RBI in 149 at-bats. (Quilici later managed the Twins from 1972 to 1975.)

4) Billy Martin

5) Three: a double by Quilici and singles by Versalles and Killebrew.

6) Lou Johnson

7) None. Harmon Killebrew and Zoilo Versalles each hit .286.

8) Two

9) Bob Allison. Bob's catch is one of the most memorable in club history, helping the team take a 2-0 series lead with the 5-1 triumph.

10) Jim Kaat

11) Jim "Mudcat" Grant, who lost Game 4 to Don Drysdale 7-2.

12) Jim Kaat

13) Sandy Koufax, who was a 19-year-old phenom pitching in his hometown of Brooklyn. Koufax was 2-2 in his initial season, but didn't pitch in the series.

14) Sam Mele, the Twins manager in the '65 World Series.

15) Claude Osteen (4-0) and Sandy Koufax (7-0)

16) 4-8. They went 0-3 in the World Series; however, they also went 4-5 playing at the Dodgers' home park during the regular-season. How? Because they played their American League rival, the Los Angeles Angels, there while their new park was being constructed in Anaheim.

17) Jim Merritt, who was from nearby Altadena, California.

18) Sandy Koufax. Twenty-nine at the time, Koufax went 2-1 with a 0.38 ERA.

19) Zoilo Versalles. The two big sluggers, Harmon Killebrew and Tony Oliva, were held to just two RBI each.

20) Ron Perranoski and Bob Miller. Perranoski became a two-time A.L. Fireman of the Year for Minnesota in 1969 and 1970 while Miller served as a middle reliever for the Twins in 1968 and 1969.

21) Dodger Stadium in the area called Chavez Ravine.

22) Jim "Mudcat" Grant.

23) Ron Fairly, who hit .379.

24) 29. He allowed just 13 hits and had an ERA of 0.38 in 24 innings.

25) Jim Lefebvre. Lefebvre's son Ryan, a former Gopher star, broadcast games from 1996-98 before leaving to work for the Kansas City Royals.

26) The Twins hit .195 as a team while the Dodgers' hit a composite .274.

27) Bob Allison, who was the tying run after a Killebrew single.

28) Willie Davis and Maury Wills; Davis stole all three bases in Game 5.

29) Earl Battey (No misprint; the slow-footed catcher hit just .120 (3-25) in the World Series.

30) Harmon Killebrew and Tony Oliva

31) 3B– Jim Gilliam, SS- Maury Wills, 2B- Jim Lefebvre, and 1B– Wes Parker.

21

WORLD SERIES 1987

1) What two Twins hitters slammed grand slams in the '87 World Series, the first teammates to do so in one Series since Yogi Berra and Moose Skowron of the Yankees' connected in 1956?

2) How many switch-hitters did the N.L. champion St. Louis Cardinals have in their starting lineup?

3) What Twins starter had the highest batting average among players who played in every game of the series?

4) Who was voted the Most Valuable Player of the '87 World Series?

5) What key Cardinals player was injured and unavailable to play in the 1987 World Series, a serious blow to the N.L. champions?

6) Besides Frank Viola's two victories, who were the two other Twins pitchers to gain World Series wins?

7) Who was the skipper for the 1987 St. Louis Cardinals', a man who had managed several years against the Twins as the manager of the Royals?

8) The Twins became the first World Series champion to accomplish what feat?

9) When St. Louis won Games 3, 4, and 5 in their own ballpark, how many runs did the Twins score in those three consecutive defeats?

10) The Metrodome became either famous or infamous during the 1987 post-season when the Minneapolis Star Tribune promoted the use of what promotional souvenir?

11) What Cardinals' outfielder led the team with 10 hits but also grounded out to make the final out of the '87 World Series?

Kirby Puckett

12) What Twins player, who hit .412 during the Series, had the game-winning RBI in Game 6?

13) What three Twins pitchers batted for the team in St. Louis in 1987?

14) The two Cardinals that homered in the 1987 World Series both had the same first name. Who were they?

15) What two Twins fielders combined to make the final defensive play in Game 7 of the '87 Series?

16) In Game 6 in Minneapolis, with the Twins down three games to two and trailing 5-3 in the fifth inning, what batter slammed a two-run homer to tie the score?

17) Who was credited with the game-winning RBI in Game 7 of the '87 Series when his 6th-inning bases-loaded infield single scored the go-ahead run?

18) What Twins regular collected four hits and scored four runs in Game 6 as the Twins knotted the Series at 3-3?

19) How many saves did Twins closer Jeff Reardon have in the World Series in 1987?

20) What Cards' rookie started both Games 1 and 7?

21) What three Twins hitters led the team with five runs scored in '87?

22) What Cardinals catcher led the team in hitting among players who appeared in all seven games?

23) How many games over .500 were the Twins in the 1987 regular-season?

24) What member of the Twins starting rotation started twice in the 1987 Series and came away with two non-decisions?

25) What right-handed reliever for the Twins lost Game 3 in St. Louis when the Cardinals rallied for three runs in the 6th inning to win 3-1 and cut the Twins lead to 2-1?

26) What Cardinals' executive lost huge sums of money in the stock market crash that occurred during the series?

27) An incredibly swift team but lacking power, how many extra-base hits did the Cardinals' total in the '87 Series?

28) Who led the Twins in RBI in the '87 World Series?

29) How high did the peak decibel meter reach during the home games at the Metrodome during the '87 World Series?

30) What recreational activity was Twins first baseman Kent Hrbek involved in on the morning of Sunday, October 25, 1987, the date of Game 7 of the World Series?

◀ *Answers to Chapter 21* ▶

1) Dan Gladden (Game 1) and Kent Hrbek (Game 6)

2) Five. CF- Willie McGee, 2B- Tommy Herr, SS – Ozzie Smith, LF – Vince Coleman, 3B and OF – Jose Oquendo. Third-baseman Terry Pendleton was also a switch-hitter but due to injury, he batted only right-handed in limited duty (3-7).

3) Kirby Puckett hit .357 (10-28).

4) Frank Viola. "Sweet Music" won Games 1 and 7 and struck out 16 hitters in 19 innings and walked just three batters.

5) Jack Clark. The Cardinals' slugging first-baseman had 35 homers and 106 RBI in just 131 games and led the N.L. in walks.

6) Bert Blyleven (game 2) and Dan Schatzeder (game 6)

7) Dorrel "Whitey" Herzog. "Whitey" managed in three World Series, winning the '82 Series 4-3 over Milwaukee and losing 4-3 to both Kansas City and Minnesota, in '85 and '87, respectively.

8) Win all four games at home to win the World Series. They also did it in 1991 against Atlanta.

9) Five. The Cardinals won 3-1, 7-2, and 4-2 in games 3, 4, and 5.

10) "Homer Hankies"

11) Willie McGee

12) Steve Lombardozzi, who was 7-17 in the Series.

13) Bert Blyleven (0-1), Les Straker (0-2), and Frank Viola (0-1)

14) Tommy Herr and Tom Lawless

15) Gary Gaetti, at third base, fielded a ground ball and tossed it to Kent Hrbek at first base to win Minnesota's first World Series title.

16) Don Baylor, who was acquired for the stretch run and went 5 for 13 (.385) in the Fall Classic, played just 20 regular-season games for the club.

17) Greg Gagne

18) Kirby Puckett

19) One (Game 7); Reardon had saved 31 games during the regular campaign.

20) Joe Magrane, who lost Game 1. Danny Cox relieved to lose Game 7.

21) Greg Gagne, Kirby Puckett, and Tom Brunansky.

22) Tony Pena (.409 on 9-22)

23) Eight. The Twins were 85-77 (.525). The only World Series winner with a worse record were the 2006 St. Louis Cardinals, who were 83-78 (.516).

24) Les Straker. The right-hander, who was the team's number three starter behind Viola and Blyleven, started Games 3 and 6.

25) Juan Berenguer

26) Cardinals' owner August Busch

27) 10. The Cards' had just two homers, no triples, and 8 doubles while the Twins totaled 20 extra-base hits.

28) Dan Gladden (7)

29) 110. The decibel meter measuring device used by ABC actually broke.

30) Duck hunting

22

WORLD SERIES 1991

1) Who was the manager of the National League champion Atlanta Braves?

2) Who became just the second team to win the World Series by winning all four of their home games?

3) What Edina East High product was the starting catcher for Atlanta in the 1991 World Series?

4) The 1991 Series between the Twins and Braves was one of the most hotly-contested in history. How many games went to extra innings?

5) What Twins pitcher became the first pitcher to pinch-hit in a World Series since Don Drysdale against the Twins in 1965?

6) Who were the winning and losing pitchers in Game 1 of the '91 Series? (Hint: both played more dramatic roles later in the series.)

7) What unusual occurrence did Atlanta and Minnesota share as opponents in the '91 Series?

8) What Atlanta third-baseman, the N.L. MVP in 1991, led the team in hits (11) and runs (6) in the Series?

9) Which player for Atlanta saw World Series action with four different teams during his career?

10) Who other than Jack Morris earned wins for the victorious Twins in the 1991 Fall Classic?

11) Did Twins first-baseman Kent Hrbek have a higher batting average in the World Series in 1987 or 1991?

12) How many of the 1991 World Series games were one-run contests?

Kent Hrbek

13) In the Series' most controversial play, what Atlanta player was tagged out at first base by Minnesota's Kent Hrbek in Game 2, after the burly fielder apparently tugged him off the base?

14) The outcome of the Twins' first two home games of the 1991 series resembled those of the 1965 and 1987 Series in what respect?

15) What Braves' hitter bounced into a first-home-first double play with the bases loaded to end the 8th inning of Game 7?

16) What young Braves' righthander recorded a 1.26 ERA in two starts, including 7⅓ innings of shutout ball in Game 7, without a decision?

17) Who pitched two shutout innings to record the win for the Twins when Kirby Puckett homered off Charlie Leibrandt in the 11th inning of Game 6 in the '91 Series?

18) Kirby Puckett's leaping grab against the plexiglas in left-center field prevented what Atlanta hitter from getting an extra-base hit in Game 6 of the '91 Series?

19) How did Twins infielders Chuck Knoblauch and Greg Gagne fake out Atlanta's Lonnie Smith as he rounded second-base in the 8th inning of Game 7, saving a run (and the Series!)?

20) Which Twins homered more than once in the '91 Series?

21) What Twins batter, among those who played at a starting position throughout the 1991 Series, led the club in batting average?

22) What was the record for the home teams in the '91 World Series?

23) Who was the pitcher who gave up Gene Larkin's game-winning single in the 10th inning of Game 7?

24) What Twins rookie belted a game-winning homer in the 8th inning to win Game 2 by a score of 3-2 at the Metrodome?

25) In one of his best post-season performances, which Twins player had three hits, three RBI, and two runs scored in Game 6 of the '91 Series?

26) What diminutive Braves' second-baseman led Atlanta with a .417 average, including three triples?

27) Which Twins player led the team with five runs scored in the '91 World Series, including the eventual game-winner in Game 7?

28) Which team outscored the other 29-24 and out-hit the other .253 to .232 in the closely-fought 1991 contest?

29) What Twins starter, who led the team in regular-season wins with 20, started two games in the Series without a decision?

30) What was the famous call made by TV broadcaster Jack Buck when Kirby Puckett hit his game-winning home-run in Game 6?

31) When was the last time that the Senators/Twins franchise won a road game in the World Series?

1) Bobby Cox. The former Yankees' infielder led Atlanta to 14 division titles in 15 years from 1991-2005, including 11 straight at one point. (In 1994, due to a player's strke, no division winners were declared.) However, Cox won only one World Series in all those trips to the post-season, a 4-2 Series victory over Cleveland in 1995.

2) Minnesota Twins (1991). The Twins were also the first to do so in 1987.

3) Greg Olson. The former Gopher star started his career with the Twins late in 1989, catching three games and going 1-2 before joining Atlanta the following year and hitting .262 as the starting backstop.

4) Three. Games, 3, 6, and 7 all went beyond regulation. Atlanta won game 3 in the 12th inning 5-4; Minnesota won game 6 in the 11th inning 4-3, and also the final game in the 10th inning 1-0.

5) Rick Aguilera. He lined out to deep center field in the top of the 12th inning with the score tied 4-4 and the bases loaded.

6) WP – Jack Morris; LP – Charlie Leibrandt. Morris would go on to be the M.V.P. after crafting his 1-0 10-inning masterpiece in Game 7 and Leibrandt went on to give up Kirby Puckett's game-winning homer in Game 6.

7) Atlanta and Minnesota became the first teams to ever reach a World Series after finishing in last place the previous year (1990).

8) Terry Pendleton

9) Lonnie Smith. The much-traveled Smith played in the World Series for Philadelphia (1980), St. Louis (1982), Kansas City (1985), and Atlanta (1991 and 1992)

10) Kevin Tapani (Game 2) and Rick Aguilera (Game 6).

11) 1987. Hrbek hit .208 (5-24) in '87 but only .115 (3-26) in '91.

12) 5. Only Game 1 (5-2 for Minnesota) and Game 5 (Atlanta 14-5) were not decided by a single tally.

13) Ron Gant

14) The Twins swept the first two games.

171

15) Sid Bream

16) John Smoltz, who became one of baseball's best clutch pitchers.

17) Rick Aguilera

18) Ron Gant

19) After Smith singled, Terry Pendleton doubled to deep left center field. Both Knobloch and Gagne pretended it was a ground ball. Smith hesitated, headed back to second briefly, and only made it to third on a hit he could easily have scored on.

20) Chili Davis and Kirby Puckett both hit two homers.

21) Brian Harper (.381; 8-21)

22) 7-0. The Twins won Games 1, 2, 6, and 8 at home and Atlanta won Games 3, 4, and 5 at home.

23) Alejandro Pena

24) Scott Leius

25) Kirby Puckett

26) Mark Lemke

27) Dan Gladden

28) Atlanta

29) Scott Erickson

30) "Deep to left center....And we'll see ya' tomorrow night."

31) Oct. 7, 1925. The Senators, with Walter Johnson pitching, beat Pittsburgh in Game 1 of the '25 Series. Since then, Washington lost three straight in 1925 and two straight in the 1933 Series. In the 1965 Series, the Twins lost all three in Los Angeles. In '87, they lost all three at St. Louis, and then dropped all three in Atlanta in '91. All told, they are on a 14-game losing streak.

23

POTPOURRI

1) What man who is currently a P.A. announcer for Gopher baseball and basketball games, worked as an usher at Met Stadium and had the opportunity to drive the bullpen car?

2) What Twins batter made the last out at Metropolitan Stadium?

3) What Twin Cities-area financial institution sponsored a contest in which any batter who hit a ball against their large advertisement beyond the bullpens in right-center field at Met Stadium would receive $50,000?

4) For which season did the Twins sell the most season tickets?

5) Who did Gene Larkin pinch-hit for in Game 7 of the 1991 World Series when he delivered a clutch single to knock in Dan Gladden with the winning run in the 10th inning to give the home team the thrilling 1-0 victory?

6) In what year did the Twins alternate back and forth between two managers, and who were they?

7) How many of his 573 career homers did Harmon Killebrew *not* hit in a Twins uniform?

8) How many times have the Twins been on the losing side of either a no-hitter or a perfect game?

9) What is the name of the Twins spring training facility in Ft. Myers, Florida?

10) What Twins pitcher allowed two inside-the-park home runs to the same hitter in the same game?

11) What three Baseball Hall of Fame members ended their careers in a Twins uniform?

12) What Twins player was responsible for popularizing the protective flap that became commonplace on all batting helmets by the late 1960's after suffering two broken cheekbones from pitched balls? And who was the Twins equipment manager who designed the flap?

13) Which is the only Minnesota city to serve as a minor-league affiliate for the Twins?

14) What six Hall of Fame players played at least a part of one season with the Twins?

15) Who are the only native Minnesotan hurlers to win 20 games in a single season for the Twins?

16) What cities have served as the location for the Twins AAA minor-league team from 1961-2009?

Gary Gaetti

17) In Kent Hrbek's first game, he homered in the 12th inning to win a game at Yankee Stadium in August of 1981. Who was the Yanks' pitcher who gave up Hrbek's first major-league roundtripper?

18) Who did the Twins trade to Cleveland in May of 1963 for Indians pitcher Jim Perry, who went on to win the 1970 Cy Young award for Minnesota?

19) Which of Calvin Griffith's relatives married former Washington Senator great Joe Cronin, who later became the American League President?

20) For which Twins opener did some players have to be delivered to the game by helicopter after spring floods ravaged roads?

21) Who were the catchers on the four occasions when a Twins pitcher recorded a no-hitter?

22) Who among Twins draft choices were selected first overall in the baseball draft? (Hint: One never signed with the Twins.

23) What Twin had pinch-hit earlier in his career for Roger Maris and Hall of Famers Carl Yastrzemski and Ted Williams?

24) Which former Twins have gone on to manage other teams to World Series victory?

25) Before the Twins moved their spring training home to Ft. Myers in 1991, in what city did the Twins train and at what field?

26) Only one pitcher to wear a Twins uniform has won more than 20 games against Minnesota. Who is he?

27) Who among Twins hurlers have had back-to-back 20-win seasons?

28) Who leads the Twins in all-time pinch-hits?

29) What team has the Twins faced most often on Opening Day?

30) Only two Twins batters other than Harmon Killebrew have won an A.L. RBI crown. Who were they?

31) Did Harmon Killebrew have more walks or strikeouts during his 22-year career?

32) Who are the only Twins hitters besides Rod Carew (.334), Joe Mauer (.327), Kirby Puckett (.318), and Tony Oliva (.304) to hold at least a .300 batting average while with the Twins (minimum 1,500 at-bats)?

33) How many American League batting titles have Twins hitters won?

34) During what decade did the Twins have the best win-loss percentage?

35) What do the following Twins have in common: Bert Blyleven, Paul Ratliff, and Jim Manning?

36) What is the last name of legendary Twins vendor Wally The Beerman?

37) When Paul Molitor became the 21st player to collect his 3,000th hit at Kansas City on Sept. 16, 1996, he was the first to do so with what type of hit?

38) What two players have topped Rod Carew's 1977 .388 batting average in more recent times?

39) How many times did slick-fielding first baseman Kent Hrbek earn a Gold Glove award in his 13-year career?

40) How old was Andy MacPhail when he was promoted to General Manager of the Twins in August 1985?

41) Who are the only Twins players to be members of both the 1987 and the 1991 World Series championship teams?

42) When Kirby Puckett retired, he had the highest career batting average for a right-handed batter since what player who retired 44 years earlier?

43) What were the three primary positions played by Harmon Killebrew for the Twins?

44) A day after establishing a major-league record by executing two triple plays at Boston on July 17, 1990, what other fielding record did the Twins and Red Sox tie?

45) How many games did Harmon Killebrew play for the Washington Senators in his first five seasons (1954-58)?

46) When questioned about his defensive prowess as a shortstop with the Twins in the early 1970's, what did Danny Thompson say his number "5" should be changed to?

47) What former Twins player and present National League manager said that Harmon Killebrew once told him not to chew gum while he was hitting because it would make his eyeballs bounce up and down?

48) What two colleges did Kirby Puckett attend before being signed by the Twins in 1982?

49) Only two major-league pitchers have pitched more seasons in the majors than Jim Kaat, who pitched for 25 seasons, 13 with Minnesota. Can you name them?

50) What scout, a former Washington Senators' star third-baseman himself, signed Harmon Killebrew in 1954 out of Payette, Idaho?

51) The same pitcher earned the win when the Twins won their 1,000th and 2,000th games. Who was he?

52) What sized-bat did Twins great Rod Carew use during most of his career?

53) What Twins player became the first major-league player to earn $3 million a year after the 1989 season?

54) Which state has produced the most Twins players with 118 (about 1/6 of the total of 660 players from 1961-2009)?

55) What World Series' winning manager once led the Twins in pinch-hits in two different seasons?

56) Which month is the Twins' best for win-loss percentage?

57) What is the Twins record on Opening Day?

58) Bert Blyleven ranks in the top ten in two major categories among major-league pitchers? What are they ?

59) Which Twins player, a 52nd round draft choice in 1989, ended up playing 11 seasons for the team (876 games) from 1993-03; he also is the father of "twins?

60) Through 2009, do the Twins have a winning or losing record?

61) What college did both Dan Gladden and Matt Garza star for?

62) Who is the tallest player ever to play for the Twins?

63) The Twins have had players from 18 different countries on their roster over the years. What two countries have each produced 16?

64) In what season did the Twins own their best-ever record at home?

65) What Twins batter had the team's first-ever inside-the-park homer on July 4, 1961?

66) In 1963, the Twins became the first major-league team to measure what?

67) How many of the Twins first-round choices in the annual June draft (since 1965) have actually played for Minnesota?

68) Who is the only person to serve as player, coach, manager, and radio announcer for the Twins organization?

69) What were the words to the first stanza of the Twins original theme song created by Dick Wilson for the Twins inaugural season in 1961?

70) What is the overall home and road winning percentage for the Twins from 1961-2009?

◀ *Answers to Chapter 23* ▶

1) Dick Jonckowski

2) Roy Smalley, who popped out to Royals shortstop U. L. Washington in the Twins 5-2 loss to Kansas City on Sept. 30, 1981.

3) Midwest Federal. Can anyone ever forget those Hal Greenwood ads?

4) 2010

5) Jarvis Brown, a reserve outfielder.

6) 1961; Cookie Lavagetto, then Sam Mele, back to Lavagetto, then back to Mele. Mele remained the manager until being fired in 1967.

7) 98. Killebrew hit 573 lifetime homers but he hit 84 with the Senators from 1954-1960 and finished with 14 homers for Kansas City in 1975.

8) Four. The Twins have suffered perfect-game losses to Oakland's Catfish Hunter in 1968 and the Yankees' David Wells in 1998. No-hitters against them include Oakland's Vida Blue (1971) and the Angels' Nolan Ryan (1974).

9) Hammond Stadium in Lee County Sports Complex. It was first utilized in 1991, when the Twins had their best-ever spring training record. They went on, of course, to win their second World Series title that October.

10) Bert Blyleven. Slugger Dick Allen of the White Sox collected two inside-the-park homers on July 31, 1972. Allen hit a three-run homer in the first inning and a two-run shot in the fifth as the Sox won 8-1. Both balls were hit to centerfield.

11) Steve Carlton (1988), Kirby Puckett (1995), and Paul Molitor (1996)

12) Earl Battey, Twin catcher; equipment manager, Ray Crump.

13) The St. Cloud Rox were a Class-A farm club from 1965 to 1970.

14) Steve Carlton (1987, 88); Dave Winfield (1993-94), Rod Carew (1967-1978), Harmon Killebrew (1961-1974); Kirby Puckett (1984-95) and Paul Molitor (1996-98).

15) Dave Goltz (20-11 in 1977) and Jerry Koosman (20-17 in 1979).

16) Rochester, N.Y. (2003-2009); Edmonton, Alberta, Canada (2001-02); Salt Lake City (1994-2000); Portland, Oregon (1987-93); Toledo, Ohio (1978-86); Tacoma, Washington (1972-77); Portland, Oregon (1971); Evansville, Indiana (1970); Denver, Colorado (1965-69); Atlanta, Georgia (1964); Dallas-Ft. Worth (1962-63); Syracuse, N.Y. (1961)

17) George Frazier, who later pitched for the Twins in 1986 and 1987.

18) Jack Kralick. Kralick had pitched the team's first no-hitter the previous August in a 1-0 gem over Kansas City in Bloomington.

19) Mildred, his older sister. She was the personal secretary of Clark Griffith, Calvin's uncle and the founding owner of the franchise.

20) 1965. An incredible flood made the Minnesota River impassable.

21) Earl Battey (Jack Kralick, 1962); Jerry Zimmerman (Dean Chance, 1967); Matt Walbeck (Scott Erickson, 1991); Terry Steinbach (Eric Milton, 1999)

22) Joe Mauer (2001) and Tim Belcher (1983). Belcher never signed with Minnesota but did have a solid major league career.

23) Carroll Hardy. Hardy played in just 11 games for the Twins in 1967 and was 3-7 as a pinch-hitter. Hardy also played for the NFL 49ers.

24) Billy Martin (Yankees – 1977); Joe Altobelli (Orioles – 1983); Charlie Manuel (Phillies – 2008). Both Martin and Altobelli played for the Twins in 1961 and Manuel from 1969-72.

25) Orlando, Florida at Tinker Field (adjacent to the Citrus Bowl).

26) Jack Morris

27) Jim Perry (20-6 in 1969 and 24-12 in 1970) and Camilo Pascual (20-11 in 1962 and 21-9 in 1963).

28) Randy Bush had 74. Chip Hale (57) and Rich Reese (42) are next.

29) Oakland (12)

30) Larry Hisle (119 in 1977) and Kirby Puckett (112 in 1994)

31) Strikeouts. Harmon struck out 1,699 times and walked 1,559 times.

32) Paul Molitor (.312), Shane Mack (.309), Chuck Knoblauch (.304), and Brian Harper (.306).

33) 14 titles. Carew won seven, Oliva and Mauer three each, and Puckett one.

34) The 1960's had the highest winning percentage at .539. The 1990's were worst at .463%. Second-best was the 2000's with a .535 win percentage.

35) They were all teenagers when they made their debut for Minnesota.

36) McNeil. Wally has sold beer at Twins games for 40 years (1970-2009).

37) Triple. By the way, the first to get his 3,000th with a homer was Wade Boggs of Tampa Bay.

38) George Brett (.390 in 1980) and Tony Gywnn (.394 in 1994).

39) None. Voting is done by the league's managers and coaches.

40) 33

41) Randy Bush, Dan Gladden, Greg Gagne, Kent Hrbek, Gene Larkin, Al Newman, and Kirby Puckett.

42) Joe DiMaggio. Puckett finished with a .318 career mark while DiMaggio finished his career (1936-1951) with a .325 average.

43) First base (982 games); third base (517 games); left field (466 games). Killebrew played almost exclusively in left field from 1962-64.

44) Combined double plays for two teams with 10 in a 9-inning game. The Twins had six on defense and the Sox had four in a 5-4 Boston win.

45) 113 games. Harmon had just 254 at-bats and 11 homers as a very part-time player and was also in the minors during that time.

46) E-6. In fact, he called his autobiography *E-6, The Diary of a Major-League Shortstop*.

47) Charlie Manuel

48) Triton Community College and Bradley University

49) Nolan Ryan (27) and Tommy John (26). Kaat is one of twenty-six players to play in four decades. (Two have played in five!)

50) Ossie Bluege

51) Bert Blyleven (July 12, 1972 and Sept. 25, 1985)

52) 33 ounces and 34 inches

53) Kirby Puckett, who signed a three-year $9 million deal on Nov. 22 that year.

54) California (118 players). Ohio and Illinois are next with 31 each with New York (29) and Minnesota (27) following.

55) Charlie Manuel (1970 and 1972)

56) July (.513); 685 wins and 648 losses. April is the worst at .490.

57) 24 wins and 25 losses (1961-2009)

58) Strikeouts (5th with 3,701) and shutouts (9th with 60); Bert is 11th all-time in games started with 685.

59) Denny Hocking. Denny and his wife became the parents of fraternal twins in 2000. It turned out to be his best year in the majors, too!

60) Winning. All-time, the Twins have 3,915 wins and 3,884 losses for a .502 winning percentage through the 2009 season.

61) Fresno State (California)

62) Jon Rauch, who is 6'11" and 290 pounds. The Kentucky native and right-hander was acquired from Arizona in late August, 2009 and served in the bullpen as a set-up man.

63) Cuba and the Dominican Republic. Venezuela is next with 15 and then Canada with 6 and Australia and Mexico with 5 each. The U.S. Territory of Puerto Rico has also produced 16 players.

64) 1969. The Twins had a .701 win % after going 57-24. In 1987, the club was 56-25 (.691%).

65) Harmon Killebrew (believe it or not). The "Killer" smacked a three-run homer at Met Stadium off Chicago's Cal McLish. There was no stop-watch on Harmon! Incidentally, three Twins have had three career inside-the-parks homers – Tony Oliva, Tom Brunansky, and Greg Gagne.

66) The distance on home-runs. Len Meffert, a Stillwater State Prison educational director, measured the fence lines and angles and correlated them to determine the distance from home-plate to any distance beyond the outfield fences. The Twins public-relations direction, Tom Mee, handled the process and announced it in the press box.

67) 23

68) Frank Quilici. The affable Quilici was a player (1965, 1967-70), a coach (1971-72), a manager (1972-75), and a color analyst on radio (1976-77, 1980-82).

69) "We're Gonna Win Twins, We're Gonna Score,
We're Gonna Win Twins, watch that baseball soar..."

70) Home (2,124-1,787) .543% Road (1,791-2,096) .460%

24

RECORDS: CAREER, SEASON, GAME

1) What Twins players (2) have been involved in the most triple plays with six?

2) Of the Twins four no-hit pitchers, who is the only one to hurl one on the road?

3) What Twins player set club records for both at-bats and most plate appearances in a single season?

4) In what season did Twins pinch-hitters hit an incredible .363?

5) What five Twins batters have hit three grand slams in a season?

6) What Twins rookie pitcher walked 127 batters, which still is the club record for a season?

7) Who holds the Twins club record for highest seasonal batting average as a pinch-hitter (minimum 20 at-bats)?

8) What Twins player established club records in his rookie year that still stand with 84 extra-base hits and 374 total bases?

9) What Twins infielder set a team high with 20 triples in a season?

10) What Twins player set the all-time Minnesota record for the most multi-hit games in a season with 74?

11) In 1997, who set the Twins standard with 62 stolen bases?

12) What Twins infielder established a team mark for sacrifices in a season with 25 in 1979?

13) Who holds the Minnesota Twins record for most consecutive games played with 249?

14) In 1968, which Twins regular grounded into just two double plays in 613 at-bats?

15) What expert two-strike hitter struck out just once in every 24 at-bats in a single-season?

16) What Twins star holds the season-high with 140 runs scored?

17) How many times did Rod Carew steal home in 1969, under the tutelage of fiery manager Billy Martin?

18) When he won the A.L. Most Valuable Player award in 1969, Harmon Killebrew set the club mark with how many runs-batted-in?

19) What Twins slugger holds team highs for most home runs at home and on the road in a single season? (Hint: They were done in separate seasons).

20) What three players share the club mark for most consecutive hits with nine?

21) Who is the only other player besides the legendary Harmon Killebrew to club homers in five consecutive games?

22) What Twins hitter holds the dubious team record for strike-outs in a single season?

23) In 2004, the Twins had a scoreless streak for their pitching staff that extended to 32 innings. What three pitchers pitched successive shutouts during that streak?

24) In 1988, this Twins lefty became the first Minnesota hurler to lead the American League in E.R.A?

25) What Minnesota pitcher set club records for both games started and most decisions in a single season? (Note: it was in different seasons)

26) Which Twins hitter walked five times in a single game (on May 7, 1978, versus Baltimore)?

27) On Sept. 2, 1965, outfielder Bob Allison tied a major-league record by doing what five times in a nine-inning game? (It has not been surpassed.)

28) Only four Twins have scored five runs in a game. Name them.

29) What is the Twins' high for most team runs scored in a game?

30) What Twins hitter holds the club high for most doubles in a game with four?

31) In what year did the Twins hit exactly zero (0) grand slams?

32) Which three Twins have reached base safely in 11 straight games?

33) What Twins reliever still holds the major-league mark for the most games finished in a season?

34) What Twins hitter holds the club mark for most games with four or more hits?

35) Kirby Puckett became the ninth player in major-league history to record four hits in his first big-league game on May 8, 1984. Against what team and in what stadium did he accomplish the feat?

36) What Twins player holds the season record for most doubles in a season with 47?

37) What Twins pitcher holds the club record for most victories in a season?

38) Who are the only Twins relievers to have totaled more than 200 saves?

39) Who holds the Minnesota franchise record for most sacrifices in a game?

40) Who are the only Twins hitters to have four extra-base hits in a game twice in their Minnesota career?

41) What right-hander holds the Twins' record for giving up 11 runs in a game?

42) What pitcher once committed three balks in one game, a Twins all-time high?

43) What two Twins batters share the team record for most RBI in a single game with eight?

44) What Twins reliever set a club standard for most-consecutive shutout innings pitched?

45) Who holds the single-season save record for the Twins?

46) What Twins hurler won three 1-0 decisions in a season?

47) What batter has the all-time rookie Twins record for most walks in a season?

48) What Twins player holds the top six yearly totals in walks?

49) Who is the only pitcher to spend his entire career with the Twins and play a minimum of 10 years?

50) Who holds the club record for most complete games in a season?

◀ *Answers to Chapter 24* ▶

1) Gary Gaetti and Kent Hrbek

2) Dean Chance. The right-hander no-hit Cleveland at Municipal Stadium on Aug. 25, 1967 in a 2-1 Twins win. (The Indians scored the run in the first inning on two walks, an error and a wild pirch.)

3) Kirby Puckett. The magnificent "Puck" came to the plate 744 times and totaled 691 at-bats in 1985 batting leadoff for Minnesota.

4) 1994. Clutch hitting didn't help this club, which was 50-63.

5) Bob Allison (1962); Rod Carew (1976); Kent Hrbek (1985); Kirby Puckett (1992), and Torii Hunter (2007).

6) Jim "Bluegill" Hughes

7) Scott Leius hit .444 in 1991, going 11-25. Scott hit .286 overall.

8) Tony Oliva. "Tony-O" set several rookie records in 1964, as well, that are still tops for rookies, including batting average, games, runs, hits, and doubles.

9) Cristian Guzman (20 in 2000)

10) Kirby Puckett (1989)

11) Chuck Knoblauch, who also owns the career mark with 276.

12) Rob Wilfong

13) Harmon Killebrew (1965-67)

14) Cesar Tovar. The leadoff man hit .272 in 157 games.

15) Brian Harper. He struck out just 16 times in 385 at-bats in 1989.

16) Chuck Knoblauch. The Texas A & M alumnus set the record in 1996, the same year the team set a club mark with 877 runs.

17) Seven, which ties him with Pete Reiser for second, behind Ty Cobb's record of 8, set in 1912.

18) 140. Killebrew led the league that year.

19) Harmon Killebrew. Harmon hit 29 homers at Met Stadium in 1961 and 28 dingers in opposing ballparks in 1962.

20) Tony Oliva (1967); Mickey Hatcher (1985); and Todd Walker (1998).

21) Marty Cordova (1995). Killebrew hit homers in five straight games on two separate occasions in 1970.

22) Bobby Darwin. He struck out 145 times in 513 at-bats in 1972 (more than one strikeout for every four at-bats). Darwin led the A.L. in strikeouts in '72 (145), '73 (137), and '74 (127).

23) On June 5, 6, and 7 the Twins blanked Kansas City 9-0, 4-0, and 12-0 with Brad Radke, Johan Santana, and Kyle Lohse pitching consecutive shutouts.

24) Allan Anderson (2.45)

25) Jim Kaat. In 1965 the crafty lefthander started a whopping 42 games (18-11). In 1966, he went 25-13 for 38 total decisions.

26) Roy Smalley

27) Struck out five times.

28) Rod Carew (1977); Tim Teufel (1983); Paul Molitor (1996); Luis Rivas (2002).

29) Twenty-four. Minnesota beat Detroit 24-11 on April 24, 1996, at Tiger Stadium.

30) Kirby Puckett (May 13, 1989 at Toronto)

31) 1968. In 1961, the Twins clubbed eight, their yearly high.

32) Rod Carew (1977), Chuck Knoblauch (1996), and Todd Walker (1998)

33) Mike Marshall. The barrel-chested Marshall completed 84 games for the Twins in 1979, appearing in 90 games, all but one in relief.

34) Kirby Puckett (47). Rod Carew had 42 and Tony Oliva 28.

35) California Angels at Anaheim Stadium. Puckett was 4-5 in the game.

36) Justin Morneau (2008)

37) Jim Kaat (25 wins in 1966)

38) Rick Aguilera (254 from 1989-1995) and Joe Nathan (246 from 2004-2009).

39) Bert Blyleven (3 on July 27, 1970).

40) Kirby Puckett and Corey Koskie.

41) Rick Reed (April 21, 2003 against New York; 10 were earned)

42) Joe Niekro (April 19, 1988 vs. Yankees)

43) Glenn Adams (June 26, 1977 vs. White Sox) and Randy Bush (May 20, 1989, vs. Rangers)

44) J.C. Romero. The hard-throwing lefty went 36 2/3 innings in 32 appearances from June 26-September 11, 2004 without allowing a run. Romero pitched for the Twins from 1999-2005.

45) Joe Nathan with 47 in 2009 (Eddie Guardado had 45 in 2002)

46) Bert Blyleven (1971)

47) Butch Wynegar (79 in 1976)

48) Harmon Killebrew (career high of 145 in 1969)

49) Brad Radke (12 years; 1995-2006)

50) Bert Blyleven (25 in 1973)

25

STATISTICAL CATEGORIES (1961-2009)

HITTING: Based on minimum of 1,500 at-bats

HOME RUNS

1. Harmon Killebrew — 475
2. Kent Hrbek — 293
3. Tony Oliva — 220
4. Bob Allison — 211
5. Kirby Puckett — 207
6. Gary Gaetti — 201
7. Torii Hunter — 192
8. Tom Brunansky — 163
   Justin Morneau — 163
10. Jacque Jones — 132

BATTING AVERAGE

1. Rod Carew — .334
2. Joe Mauer — .327
3. Kirby Puckett — .318
4. Paul Molitor — .312
5. Shane Mack — .309
6. Brian Harper — .306
7. Tony Oliva — .304
   Chiuck Knobluach — .304
9. A.J. Perzynski — .301
10. Shannon Stewart — .294

RUNS BATTED IN

1. Harmon Killebrew — 1,325
2. Kent Hrbek — 1,086
3. Kirby Puckett — 1,085
4. Tony Oliva — 947
5. Gary Gaetti — 758
6. Rod Carew — 733
7. Torii Hunter — 711
8. Bob Allison — 642
9. Justin Morneau — 623
10. Roy Smalley — 485

HITS

1. Kirby Puckett — 2,304
2. Rod Carew — 2,085
3. Tony Oliva — 1,917
4. Kent Hrbek — 1,749
5. Harmon Killebrew — 1,713
6. Gary Gaetti — 1,276
7. Torii Hunter — 1,218
8. Chuck Knoblauch — 1,197
9. Cesar Tovar — 1,164
10. Roy Smalley — 1,046
    Zoilo Versalles — 1,046

TOTAL BASES

1. Kirby Puckett — 3,453
2. Harmon Killebrew — 3,412
3. Tony Oliva — 3,002
4. Kent Hrbek — 2,976
5. Rod Carew — 2,792
6. Gary Gaetti — 2,181
7. Torii Hunter — 2,105
8. Bob Allison — 1,881
9. Chuck Knoblauch — 1,638
10. Zoilo Versalles — 1,604

RUNS SCORED

1. Harmon Killebrew — 1,072
2. Kirby Puckett — 1,071
3. Rod Carew — 950
4. Kent Hrbek — 903
5. Tony Oliva — 870
6. Chuck Knoblauch — 713
7. Torii Hunter — 672
8. Bob Allison — 648
9. Gary Gaetti — 646
   Cesar Tovar — 646

GAMES PLAYED

1. Harmon Killebrew — 1,939
2. Kirby Puckett — 1,783
3. Kent Hrbek — 1,747
4. Tony Oliva — 1,676
5. Rod Carew — 1,635
6. Gary Gaetti — 1,361
7. Bob Allison — 1,236
8. Torii Hunter — 1,234
9. Randy Bush — 1,219
10. Roy Smalley — 1,148

TRIPLES

1. Rod Carew — 90
2. Cristian Guzman — 61
3. Kirby Puckett — 57
4. Zoilo Versalles — 56
5. Chuck Knoblauch — 51
6. Tony Oliva — 48
7. Cesar Tovar — 45
8. Bob Allison — 41
9. Greg Gagne — 35
10. John Castino — 34

TOTAL AT-BATS

1. Kirby Puckett — 7,244
2. Harmon Killebrew — 6,593
3. Tony Oliva — 6,301
4. Rod Carew — 6,235
5. Kent Hrbek — 6,192
6. Gary Gaetti — 4,989
7. Torii Hunter — 4,492
8. Zoilo Versalles — 4,252
9. Cesar Tovar — 4,142
10. Roy Smalley — 3,997

STRIKEOUTS

1. Harmon Killebrew — 1,314
2. Kirby Puckett — 965
3. Gary Gaetti — 877
4. Torii Hunter — 870
5. Bob Allison — 842

STOLEN BASES

1. Chuck Knoblauch — 276
2. Rod Carew — 271
3. Cesar Tovar — 186
4. Kirby Puckett — 134
5. Torii Hunter — 126
6. Dan Gladden — 116
7. Cristian Guzman — 102
8. Matt Lawton — 96
9. Larry Hisle — 92
10. Tony Oliva — 86

DOUBLES

1. Kirby Puckett — 414
2. Tony Oliva — 329
3. Kent Hrbek — 312
4. Rod Carew — 305
5. Torii Hunter — 259
6. Gary Gaetti — 252
7. Harmon Killebrew — 232
8. Chuck Knoblauch — 210
9. Cesar Tovar — 193
10. Justin Morneau — 190

WALKS

1. Harmon Killebrew — 1,321
2. Kent Hrbek — 838
3. Bob Allison — 641
4. Rod Carew — 613
5. Roy Smalley — 549
6. Chuck Knoblauch — 513
7. Kirby Puckett — 450
8. Tony Oliva — 448
9. Matt Lawton — 408
10. Tom Brunansky — 394

6. Kent Hrbek — 798
7. Jacque Jones — 737
8. Rod Carew — 716
9. Greg Gagne — 676
10. Corey Koskie — 647

ON-BASE PERCENTAGE

1. Joe Mauer   .408
2. Rod Carew   .393
3. Chuck Knoblauch   .391
4. Matt Lawton   .379
5. Harmon Killebrew   .378
6. Steve Braun   .376
7. Korey Koskie   .373
8. Kent Hrbek   .367
9. Doug Mientkiewicz   .367
10. Lyman Bostock   .366

SLUGGING PERCENTAGE

1. Harmon Killebrew   .514
2. Justin Morneau   .501
3. Joe Mauer   .483
4. Kent Hrbek   .481
   Jimmie Hall   .481
6. Shane Mack   .479
   Don Mincher   .479
8. Kirby Puckett   .477
9. Tony Oliva   .476
10. Bob Allison   .471

PITCHING: Based on minimum of 400 innings pitched

VICTORIES

1. Jim Kaat   189
2. Bert Blyleven   149
3. Brad Radke   148
4. Jim Perry   128
5. Frank Viola   112
6. Dave Goltz   96
7. Johan Santana   93
8. Camilo Pascual   88
9. Kevin Tapani   75
10. Dave Boswell   67

LOSSES

1. Jim Kaat   152
2. Brad Radke   139
3. Bert Blyleven   138
4. Frank Viola   93
5. Jim Perry   90
6. Dave Goltz   79
7. Joe Mays   65
8. Kevin Tapani   63
9. Scott Ericson   60
10. LaTroy Hawkins   57
    Kyle Lohse   57
    Camilo Pascual   57

GAMES PITCHED

1. Eddie Guardado   648
2. Rick Aguilera   490
3. Jim Kaat   468
4. Joe Nathan   412
5. Juan Rincon   386
6. Brad Radke   378
7. Jim Perry   376
8. LaTroy Hawkins   366
9. Mike Trombley   365
10. Bert Blyleven   348

EARNED-RUN-AVERAGE

1. Joe Nathan   1.87
2. A.L. Worthington   2.62
3. Dean Chance   2.67
4. Tom Hall   3.00
5. Jim Merritt   3.03
6. Bill Campbell   3.13
7. Jim Perry   3.15
8. Johan Santana   3.22
9. Bert Blyleven   3.28
   Jim Kaat   3.28

SHUTOUTS

1. Bert Blyleven — 29
2. Jim Kaat — 23
3. Camilo Pascual — 18
4. Jim Perry — 17
5. Dean Chance — 11
   Dave Goltz — 11
7. Mudcat Grant — 10
   Brad Radke — 10
   Frank Viola — 10
10. Scott Ericson — 7
    Geoff Zahn — 7

INNINGS PITCHED

1. Jim Kaat — 2,959-⅓
2. Bert Blyleven — 2,566-⅔
3. Brad Radke — 2,451
4. Jim Perry — 1,883-⅓
5. Frank Viola — 1,772-⅔
6. Dave Goltz — 1,638
7. Johan Santana — 1,308-⅔
8. Camilo Pascual — 1,284-⅔
9. Kevin Tapani — 1,171-⅓
10. Dave Boswell — 1,036-⅓

STRIKEOUTS

1. Bert Blyleven — 2,035
2. Jim Kaat — 1,824
3. Brad Radke — 1,467
4. Johan Santana — 1,381
5. Frank Viola — 1,214
6. Jim Perry — 1,025
7. Camilo Pascual — 994
8. Dave Goltz — 887
9. Dave Boswell — 865
10. Kevin Tapani — 724

COMPLETE GAMES

1. Bert Blyleven — 141
2. Jim Kaat — 133
3. Dave Goltz — 80
4. Camilo Pascual — 72
5. Jim Perry — 61
6. Frank Viola — 54
7. Dave Boswell — 37
   Brad Radke — 37
9. Mudcat Grant — 36
   Geoff Zahn — 36

GAMES STARTED

1. Jim Kaat — 422
2. Brad Radke — 377
3. Bert Blyleven — 345
4. Frank Viola — 259
5. Jim Perry — 249
6. Dave Goltz — 215
7. Kevin Tapani — 180
8. Camilo Pascual — 179
9. Johan Santana — 175
10. Eric Milton — 165

WINNING PERCENTAGE

(Minimum 50 decisions)

1. Johan Santana (93-44) — .679
2. Camilo Pascual (88-57) — .607
3. Bill Campbell (32-21) — .604
4. Mudcat Grant (50-35) — .588
5. Jim Perry (128-90) — .587
6. Scott Baker (43-33) — .566
7. Jim Kaat (189-152) — .554
   Dave Boswell (67-54) — .554
9. Dave Goltz (96-79) — .549
10. Dean Chance (41-34) — .547

SAVES

1.	Rick Aguilera	254
2.	Joe Nathan	246
3.	Eddie Guardado	116
4.	Ron Davis	108
5.	Jeff Reardon	104
6.	A.L. Worthington	88
7.	Ron Perranoski	76
8.	Mike Marshall	54
9.	Bill Campbell	51
10.	LaTroy Hawkins	44

WALKS

1.	Jim Kaat	694
2.	Bert Blyleven	674
3.	Jim Perry	541
4.	Frank Viola	521
5.	Dave Goltz	493
6.	Dave Boswell	460
7.	Brad Radke	445
8.	Camilo Pascual	431
9.	Scott Erickson	367
10.	Johan Santana	364

HOME RUNS ALLOWED

1.	Brad Radke	326	6.	Eric Milton	149
2.	Jim Kaat	270	7.	Johan Santana	144
3.	Bert Blyleven	243	8.	Kyle Lohse	128
4.	Frank Viola	213	9.	Joe Mays	127
5.	Jim Perry	166	10.	Camilo Pascual	123

Zoilo Versalles

26

TWINS YEAR-BY-YEAR RECORDS

Year	Manager	Games	Wins	Losses	Pct.	G.B.
1961	Cookie Lavagetto	59	23	36	.389	
	Sam Mele	101	47	54	.479	
	Total	161 (1)	70	90	.437	38
1962	Sam Mele	163 (1)	91	71	.562	5
1963	Sam Mele	161	91	70	.565	13
1964	Sam Mele	163 (1)	79	83	.488	20
1965	Sam Mele	162	102	60	.630	--
1966	Sam Mele	162	89	73	.549	9
1967	Sam Mele	50	25	25	.500	
	Cal Ermer	112	66	46	.589	
	Total	164 (2)	91	71	.562	1
1968	Cal Ermer	162	79	83	.488	24
1969	Billy Martin	162	97	65	.599	--
1970	Bill Rigney	162	98	64	.605	--
1971	Bill Rigney	160	74	86	.463	26.5
1972	Bill Rigney	70	36	34	.514	
	Frank Quilici	84	41	43	.488	
	* Total	154	77	77	.500	15.5
1973	Frank Quilici	162	81	81	.500	13
1974	Frank Quilici	163 (1)	82	80	.506	8
1975	Frank Quilici	159	76	83	.478	20.5
1976	Gene Mauch	162	85	77	.525	5
1977	Gene Mauch	161	84	77	.522	17.5
1978	Gene Mauch	162	73	89	.451	19
1979	Gene Mauch	162	82	80	.506	6

*denotes season with games lost due to players' strike
Numbers in parentheses refer to tie games.

Year	Manager	Games	Wins	Losses	Pct.	G.B.
1980	Gene Mauch	125	54	71	.432	
	Johnny Goryl	36	23	13	.639	
	Total	161	77	84	.478	19.5
1981	Johnny Goryl	36	11	25	.306	
	Billy Gardner	73	30	43	.410	
	* Total	110 (1)	41	68	.376	23
1982	Billy Gardner	162	60	102	.370	33
1983	Billy Gardner	162	70	92	.432	29
1984	Billy Gardner	162	81	81	.500	3
1985	Billy Gardner	62	27	35	.435	
	Ray Miller	100	50	50	.500	
	Total	162	77	85	.475	14
1986	Ray Miller	139	59	80	.424	
	Tom Kelly	23	12	11	.522	
	Total	162	71	91	.438	21
1987	Tom Kelly	162	85	77	.525	--
1988	Tom Kelly	162	91	71	.562	13
1989	Tom Kelly	162	80	82	.494	19
1990	Tom Kelly	162	74	88	.457	29
1991	Tom Kelly	162	95	67	.586	--
1992	Tom Kelly	162	90	72	.556	6
1993	Tom Kelly	162	71	91	.438	23
1994	* Tom Kelly	113	53	60	.469	14
1995	*Tom Kelly	144	56	88	.389	44
1996	Tom Kelly	162	78	84	.481	21.5
1997	Tom Kelly	162	68	94	.420	18.5
1998	Tom Kelly	162	70	92	.432	19
1999	Tom Kelly	161 (1)	63	97	.394	33
2000	Tom Kelly	162	69	93	.426	26
2001	Tom Kelly	162	85	77	.525	6
2002	Ron Gardenhire	161	94	67	.584	--
2003	Ron Gardenhire	162	90	72	.556	--

*denotes season with games lost due to players' strike
Numbers in parentheses refer to tie games.

2004	Ron Gardenhire	162	92	70	.568	--
2005	Ron Gardenhire	162	83	79	.512	16
2006	Ron Gardenhire	162	96	66	.593	--
2007	Ron Gardenhire	162	79	83	.488	17
2008	Ron Gardenhire	163*	88	75	.540	1
2009	Ron Gardenhire	163†	87	76	.534	--

TOTAL		
	Games	**7,807** (8)
	Wins	**3,915**
	Losses	**3,884**
	Winning percentage	**.502**

* In 2008, when the regular season ended in a tie, the Twins lost a one-game playoff (1-0) to Chicago to determine the A.L. Central Championship.

†In 2009, the Twins won the division by defeating Detroit 6-5 in a one-game playoff (12 innings) to resolve another regular-season tie.

Note: In seven different seasons, there were games that were called because of rain or curfew with the score tied and later replayed in full. However, the game statistics from those tie games still count. In 1961, 1962, 1964, 1974, 1981, and 1999, the Twins played a tie game and in 1967 they played two. Thus, the Twins have played 7,807 total games counting ties and 7,799 in which they either won or lost. The number in parentheses behind the number of games played for a season indicates tie games that were later replayed.

27

COMPLETE TWINS PLAYER ROSTER (1961-2009)

Player, Years with Twins, Position

A

Paul Abbott 1990-92 RHP

Brent Abernathy 2005 2B

Glenn Adams 1977-81 OF-DH

Mike Adams 1972-72 OF

Juan Agosto 1986 LHP

Rick Aguilera 1989-99 RHP

Vic Albury 1973-76 LHP

Scott Aldred 1996-97 LHP

Bernie Allen 1962-66 2B

Chad Allen 1999-2001 OF

Bob Allison 1961-70 OF

Joe Altobelli 1961 1B

Brant Alyea 1970-71 OF

Allan Anderson 1987-1991 LHP

Danny Ardoin 2000 C

Gerry Arrigo 1961-64 LHP

Fernando Arroyo 1980-82 RHP

Keith Atherton 1986-88 RHP

Luis Ayala 2009 RHP

B

Wally Backman 1989 2B

Mike Bacsik 1979-80 RHP

Chuck Baker 1981 SS

Doug Baker 1988-90 SS

Scott Baker 2005-2009 RHP

James Baldwin 2003 RHP

Grant Balfour 2001, 03-05 RHP

Eddie Bane 1973, 1975-76 LHP

George Banks 1962-64 3B

Willie Banks 1991-93 RHP

Travis Baptist 1998 RHP

John Barnes 2000-01 OF

Steve Barber 1970-71 RHP

Jason Bartlett 2004-07 SS

Brian Bass 2008 RHP

Randy Bass 1977 1B

Tony Batista 2006 3B

Earl Battey 1961-67 C

Don Baylor 1987 OF

Billy Beane 1986-87 OF

Rich Becker 1993-97 OF

Julio Becquer 1961, '63 1B

Steve Bedrosian 1991 RHP

Joe Beimel 2004 LHP

Erik Bennett 1996 RHP

Juan Berenguer 1987-90 RHP

Sean Bergman 2000 LHP

Reno Bertoia 1961 3B

Karl Best 1988 RHP

Bill Bethea 1964 2B

Jeff Bittiger 1987 RHP

Nick Blackburn 2007-09 RHP

Casey Blake 2000-02 3B

Henry Blanco 2004 C

Bud Bloomfield 1964 2B

Bert Blyleven 1970-76, 85-88 RHP

Walt Bond 1967 OF

Joe Bonikowski 1962 RHP

Boof Bonser 2006-2008 RHP

Greg Booker 1989 RHP

Bret Boone 2005 2B

Pat Borders 2004 C

Glenn Borgmann 1972-79 C

Paul Boris 1982 RHP

Lyman Bostock 1975-77 OF

Dave Boswell 1964-70 RHP

Pat Bourque 1974 1B

Rob Bowen 2003-04 C

Shane Bowers 1997 RHP

Travis Bowyer 2005 RHP

Darrell Brandon 1969 RHP

Steve Braun 1970-76 OF

Brent Brede 1996-97 OF

Craig Breslow 2008-09 LHP

Ken Brett 1979 LHP

Johnny Briggs 1975 OF

Bernardo Brito 1992-93; '95 OF

Darrell Brown 1983-84 OF

Jarvis Brown 1991-92 OF

Mark Brown 1985 RHP

Fred Bruckbauer 1961 LHP

J.T. Bruett 1992-93 OF

Greg Brummett 1993 RHP

Tom Brunansky 1982-88 OF

Steve Brye 1970-76 OF

Brian Buchanan 2000-02 OF

Bud Bulling 1977 C

Eric Bullock 1988 OF

Tom Burgmeier 1974-77 LHP

Dennis Burtt 1985-86 RHP

Brian Buscher 2007-09 3B

Randy Bush 1982-93 OF

John Butcher 1984-86 RHP

Sal Butera 1980-82; '87 C

Bill Butler 1974-75; '77 LHP

C

Orlando Cabrera 2009 SS

Carmen Cali 2007 LHP

Bill Campbell 1973-76 RHP

Kevin Campbell 1994-95 RHP

Sal Campisi 1971 RHP

John Candelaria 1990 LHP

Jay Canizaro 2000-02 2B

Leo Cardenas 1969-71 SS

Rod Carew 1967-78 1B-2B

Steve Carlton 1987-88 LHP

Hector Carrasco 1998-2002 RHP

Don Carrrithers 1977 RHP

Larry Casian 1990-94 LHP

Alexi Casilla 2006-09 2B

Bobby Castillo 1982-84 RHP

Carmen Castillo 1989-91 OF

Luis Castillo 2006-07 2B

John Castino 1979-84 3B-2B

Juan Castro 2005-06 SS

Dean Chance 1967-69 RHP

Rich Chiles 1977-78 OF

John Christenson 1988 OF

Pete Cimino 1965-66 RHP

Jeff Cirillo 2007 3B-1B

Gerald Clark 1995 OF

Howie Clark 2008 IF

Ron Clark 1966-69 3B

Greg Colbrunn 1997 1B

Alex Cole 1994-95 OF

Jackie Collum 1962 LHP

Keith Comstock 1984 RHP

Billy Consolo 1961 SS

Mike Cook 1989 RHP

Ron Coomer 1995-2000 3B-1B

Don Cooper 1981-82 RHP

Doug Corbett 1980-82 RHP
Ray Corbin 1971-75 RHP
Tim Corcoran 1981 1B
Marty Cordova 1995-99 OF
Jesse Crain 2004-09 RHP
Joe Crede 2009 3B
Jack Cressend 2000-02 RHP
Jerry Crider 1969 RHP
Mike Cubbage, 1976-80, 3B
Michael Cuddyer 2001-09 OF
Bert Cueto 1961 RHP
Midre Cummings 1999-2000 OF

D

Bill Dailey 1963-64 RHP
Bobby Darwin 1972-75 OF
Andre David 1984, '86 OF
Cleatus Davidson 1999 2B
Mark Davidson 1986-88 OF
Chili Davis 1991-92 DH
Ron Davis 1982-86 RHP
Joe Decker 1973-76 RHP
Rick Dempsey 1969-72 C
Julio DePaula 2007 RHP
Jim Deshaies 1993-94 LHP
R.A. Dickey 2009 RHP
Dan Dobbek 1961 OF
Jim Donohue 1962 RHP
Gary Dotter 1961, '63-64 LHP
Tim Drummond 1989-90 RHP
Brian Duensing 2009 LHP
Steve Dunn 1994-95 1B
Mike Durant 1996 C
J.D. Durbin 2004 RHP
Mike Duvall 2001-02 RHP
Jim Dwyer 1988-90 OF

Mike Dyer 1989 RHP

E

Tom Edens 1991-92 RHP
Dave Edwards 1978-80 OF
Jim Eisenreich 1982-84 OF
Dave Engle 1981-85 C
Roger Erickson 1978-82 RHP
Scott Erickson 1990-95 RHP
Alvaro Espinoza 1984-86 SS
Frank Eufemia 1985 RHP
Adam Everett 2008 SS
Willie Eyre 2006 RHP

F

Lenny Faedo 1980-84 SS
Terry Felton 1979-82 RHP
Sergio Ferrer 1974-75 SS
Mike Fetters 2003 RHP
Danny Fife 1973-74 RHP
Pete Filson 1982-86 LHP
Tony Fiore 2001-03 RHP
Bill Fischer 1964 RHP
Ray Fontenot 1986 RHP
Dan Ford 1975-78 OF
Lew Ford 2003-07 OF
Mike Fornieles 1963 RHP
Jerry Fosnow 1964-65 LHP
George Frazier 1986-87 RHP
Kevin Frederick 2002 RHP
Aaron Fultz 2004 LHP
Mark Funderburk 1981, '85 OF

G

Armando Gabino 2009 RHP
Gary Gaetti 1981-90 3B

Greg Gagne 1983-92 SS
Rich Garces 1990, '93 RHP
Billy Gardner 1961 2B
Keith Gargozzo 1994 LHP
Matt Garza 2006-07 RHP
Dave Gassner 2005 LHP
Brent Gates 1989-90 2B-3B
Bob Gebhard 1971-72 RHP
Paul Giel 1961 RHP
Dan Gladden 1987-91 OF
Dave Goltz 1972-79 RHP
Carlos Gomez 2008-09 OF
Chris Gomez 2003 IF
Luis Gomez 1974-77 SS
Ruben Gomez 1962 RHP
German Gonzalez 1988-89 RHP
Danny Goodwin 1979-81 1B
Bob Gorinski 1977 OF
Johnny Goryl 1962-64 2B
Mauro Gozzo 1992 RHP
Dan Graham 1979 3B
Wayne Granger 1972 RHP
Mudcat Grant 1964-67 RHP
Lenny Green 1961-64 OF
Seth Greisinger 2004 RHP
Joe Grzenda 1969 LHP
Eddie Guardado 1993-2003; 2008 LHP
Matt Guerrier 2004-09 RHP
Bucky Guth 1972 SS
Mark Guthrie 1989-95 LHP
Cristian Guzman 1999-2004 SS

H
Chip Hale 1989-90; 93-96 2B
Jimmie Hall 1963-66 OF

Tommy Hall 1968-71 LHP
Pete Hamm 1970-71 RHP
Bill Hands 1973-74 RHP
Greg Hansell 1996 RHP
Carroll Hardy 1967 OF
Brian Harper 1988-93 C
Brendan Harris 2008-09 IF
Greg Harris 1995 RHP
Roric Harrison 1978 RHP
Mike Hart 1984 OF
Mike Hartley 1993 RHP
Paul Hartzell 1979 RHP
Mickey Hatcher 1981-86 OF, IF
Brad Havens 1981-83 LHP
LaTroy Hawkins 1995-2003 RHP
Hal Haydel 1970-71 RHP
Neal Heaton 1986 LHP
Chris Heintz 2005-07 C
Sean Henn 2009 LHP
Ron Henry 1961, '64 C
Jackie Hernandez 1967-68 SS
Livan Hernandez 2008 RHP
Tom Herr 1988 2B
Donny Hill 1992 IF
Herman Hill 1969-70 OF
Larry Hisle 1973-77 OF
John Hobbs 1981 LHP
Denny Hocking 1993-2003 IF, OF
Ed Hodge 1984 LHP
Dave Hollins 1996 3B
Jeff Holly 1977-79 LHP
Jim Holt 1968-74 OF
Vince Horsman 1995 LHP
Steve Howe 1985 LHP
Kent Hrbek 1981-94 1B
Justin Huber 2009 DH

Jim Hughes 1974-77 RHP
Philip Humber 2008 RHP
Randy Hundley 1974 C
Torii Hunter 1997-2007 OF
Butch Huskey 2000 OF

I

Ricardo Ingram 1995 OF
Hank Izquierdo 1967 C

J

Darrell Jackson 1978-82 LHP
Darrin Jackson 1997 OF
Mike Jackson 2002 RHP
Ron Jackson 1979-81 1B
Roy Lee Jackson 1986 RHP
Lamar Jacobs 1961 OF
Kevin Jarvis 1997 RHP
Marcus Jensen 2000 C
Houston Jimenez 1983-84 SS
Adam Johnson 2001,'03 RHP
Dave Johnson 1977-78 RHP
Randy Johnson 1982 OF
Tom Johnson 1974-78 RHP
Greg Johnston 1980-81 OF
Garrett Jones 2007 1B-OF
Jacque Jones 1999-2005 OF
Todd Jones 2001 RHP
Ryan Jorgensen 2008 C
Terry Jorgensen 1989,'92-93 3B

K

Jim Kaat 1961-73 LHP
Ron Keller 1966,'68 RHP
Pat Kelly 1967-68 OF
Roberto Kelly 1996-97 OF

Tom Kelly 1975 1B
Bobby Keppel 2009 RHP
Bobby Kielty 2001-03 OF
Harmon Killebrew 1961-74
    1B,3B,OF
Jerry Kindall 1964-65 2B
Matt Kinney 2000; 02 RHP
Mike Kinnunen 1980 LHP
Bob Kipper 1992 LHP
Tom Klawitter 1985 LHP
Ron Kline 1967 RHP
Scott Klingenbeck 1995-96 RHP
Joe Klink 1987 LHP
Johnny Klippstein 1964-66 RHP
Chuck Knoblauch 1991-97 2B
Jerry Koosman 1979-81 LHP
Bobby Korecky 2008 RHP
Andy Kosco 1965-67 OF
Corey Koskie 1998-2004 3B
Frank Kostro 1964-65; 67-69 OF
Jack Kralick 1961-63 LHP
Bill Krueger 1992 LHP
Jason Kubel 2004-09 OF
Rusty Kuntz 1983 OF
Craig Kusick 1973-79 1B

L

David Lamb 2002 IF
Mike Lamb 2008 3B
Ken Landreaux 1979-80 OF
Gene Larkin 1987-93 1B-OF
Dave LaRoche 1972 LHP
Fred Lasher 1963 RHP
Bill Latham 1986 RHP
Chris Latham 1997-99 OF
Tim Laudner 1981-89 C

Matt Lawton 1995-2001 OF
Charlie Lea 1988 RHP
Terry Leach 1990-91 RHP
Matthew LeCroy 2000-05; 2007 C
Derek Lee 1993 OF
Don Lee 1961-62 RHP
Scott Leius 1990-95 3B
Jim Lemon 1961-63 OF
Ted Lepcio 1961 3B
Jim Lewis 1983 RHP
Mike Lincoln 1999-2000 RHP
Francisco Liriano 2005-09 LHP
Nelson Liriano 1990 2B
Joe Lis 1973-74 1B
Jeff Little 1982 LHP
Kyle Lohse 2001-06 RHP
Steve Lombardozzi 1995-98 2B
Bruce Look 1968 C
Dwight Lowry 1988 C
Steve Luebber 1971-72; '76 RHP
Tom Lundstedt 1975 C
Rick Lysander 1983-85 RHP

M

Kevin Maas 1995 1B
Alejandro Machado 2007 IF
Shane Mack 1990-94 OF
Pete Mackanin 1980-81 IF
Matt Macri 2008 IF
Ron Mahay 2009 LHP
Pat Mahomes 1992-96 RHP
Mike Maksudian 1993 C, 1B
Jim Manning 1962 RHP
Fred Manrique 1990 2B
Jeff Manship 2009 RHP
Charlie Manuel 1969-72 OF

Georges Marandas 1962 RHP
Mike Marshall 1979-80 RHP
Billy Martin 1961 2B
Orlando Martinez 1962 SS
Tippy Martinez 1988 LHP
Mike Mason 1988 LHP
Dan Masteller 1995 1B, OF
Joe Mauer 2004-09 C
Jason Maxwell 2001-01 2B
Joe Mays 1999-2005 RHP
Joe McCabe 1964 C
David McCarty 1993-05 1B, OF
Quinton McCracken 2001 OF
Danny McDevitt 1961 LHP
Darnell McDonald 2007 OF
David McKay 1975-76 3B
Pat Meares 1993-98 SS
David Meier 1984-85 OF
Minnie Mendoza 1970 3B
Orlando Mercado 1989 C
Orlando Merced 1998 1B, C
Brett Merriman 1993-94 RHP
Jim Merritt 1965-68 LHP
Matt Merullo 1995 C
Doug Mientkiewicz 1998-2004 1B
Jose Mijares 2008-09 LHP
Larry Milbourne 1982 2B
Mike Milchin 1996 LHP
Bob Miller 1968-69 RHP
Corky Miller 2005 C
Damian Miller 1997 C
Jason Miller 2007 LHP
Travis Miller 1996-2002 LHP
Eric Milton 1998-2003 LHP
Don Mincher 1961-66 1B
Bobby Mitchell 1982-83 OF

George Mitterwald 1966; 68-73 C
Chad Moeller 2000 C
Dustin Mohr 2001-03 OF
Paul Molitor 1996-98 DH, 1B
Craig Monroe 2008 DH, OF
Dan Monzon 1972-73 IF
Ray Moore 1961-63 RHP
Jose M. Morales 1978-80 C, DH
Jose G. Morales 2007, 2009 C
Mike Morgan 1998 RHP
Jose Morillo 2009 RHP
Justin Morneau 2003-09 1B
Danny Morris 1968-69 RHP
Jack Morris 1991 RHP
Warren Morris 2002 IF
John Moses 1988-90 OF
Danny Mota 2000 RHP
Terry Mulholland 2004-05 LHP
Kevin Mulvey 2009 RHP
Oscar Munoz 1995 RHP
Pedro Munoz 1990-95 OF
Greg Myers 1996-97 C

N
Michael Nakamura 2003 RHP
Hal Naragon 1961-62 C
Cotton Nash 1969-70 1B
Joe Nathan 2004-09 RHP
Dan Naulty 1996-98 RHP
Danny Neagle 1991 LHP
Mel Nelson 1965, '67 RHP
Pat Neshek 2006 -08 RHP
Graig Nettles 1967-69 3B, OF
Jim Nettles 1970-72 OF
Phil Nevin 2006 DH
Al Newman 1987-91 2B

Joe Niekro 1987-88 RHP
Randy Niemann 1987 LHP
Chuck Nieson 1964 RHP
Tom Nieto 1987-88 C
Otis Nixon 1988 OF
Russ Nixon 1966-67 C
Tom Norton 1972 RHP
Willie Norwood 1977-80 OF
Joe Nossek 1964-66 OF

O
Alex Ochoa 1998 OF
Jack O'Connor 1981-84 LHP
Bryan Oelkers 1983 LHP
Jose Offerman 2004 IF
Augie Ojeda 2004 IF
Tony Oliva 1962-76 OF, DH
Francisco Oliveras 1989 RHP
Jim Ollom 1966-67 LHP
Greg Olson 1989 C
Gregg Olson 1997 RHP
Jesse Orosco 2003 LHP
David Ortiz 1997-2002 1B
Junior Ortiz 1990-91 C
Ramon Ortiz 2007 RHP

P
John Pacella 1982 RHP
Mike Pagliarulo 1991-93 3B
Ed Palmquist 1961 RHP
Derek Parks 1992-94 C
Jose Parra 1995-96 RHP
Camilo Pascual 1961-66 RHP
Larry Pashnick 1984 RHP
Frank Pastore 1986 RHP
Carl Pavano 2009 RHP

Mike Pazik 1975-77 LHP
Dan Perkins 1999 RHP
Glenn Perkins 2006-09 LHP
Sam Perlozzo 1977 2B
Ron Perranoski 1968-71 LHP
Jim Perry 1963-72 RHP
Stan Perzanowski 1978 RHP
Jay Pettibone 1983 RHP
A.J. Pierzynski 1998-2003 C
Chris Pittaro 1986-87 2B
Bill Pleis 1961-66 LHP
Mike Poepping 1975 OF
Sidney Ponson 2007 RHP
Mark Portugal 1985-88 RHP
Wally Post 1963 OF
Hosken Powell 1978-81 OF
Paul Powell 1971 OF
Vic Power 1962-64 1B
Jason Pridie 2008 OF
Alex Prieto 2003-04 IF
Tom Prince 2001-03 C
Kirby Puckett 1983-95 OF
Carlos Pulido 1994; 2003 LHP
Nick Punto 2004-09 IF
Pat Putnam 1984 1B

Q
Frank Quilici 1965; '67-70 2B
Tom Quinlan 1996 3B
Luis Quinones 1992 IF

R
Brian Raabe 1995-96 2B
Josh Rabe 2006-07 OF
Brad Radke 1995-2006 RHP
Rob Radlosky 1999 RHP

Pedro Ramos 1961 RHP
Bob Randall 1976-80 2B
Gary Rath 1999 LHP
Paul Ratliff 1963; 1970-71 C
Jon Rauch 2009 RHP
Shane Rawley 1989 LHP
Jeff Reardon 1987-89 RHP
Jeff Reboulet 1992-96 IF
Pete Redfern 1976-82 RHP
Mark Redman 1999-2001 LHP
Mike Redmond 2005 -09 C
Darren Reed 1992 OF
Jeff Reed 1984-86 C
Rick Reed 2001-03 RHP
Rich Reese 1964-73 1B
Rick Renick 1968-72 3B
Michael Restovich 2002-04 OF
Dennys Reyes 2006-08 LHP
Juan Rincon 2001-08 RHP
Todd Ritchie 1997-98 RHP
Luis Rivas 2000-05 2B
Bombo Rivera 1978-80 OF
Joe Roa 2004 RHP
Rich Robertson 1995-97 LHP
Frank Rodriguez 1995-98 RHP
Jose Rodriguez 2002 LHP
Luis Rodriguez 2005-07 IF
Vic Rodriguez 1989 3B
Kenny Rogers 2003 LHP
Gary Roggenburk 1963; '65-66 LHP
Jim Roland 1962-64; 66-68 LHP
Rich Rollins 1961-68 3B
J.C. Romero 1999-2005 LHP
Phil Roof 1971-76 C
John Roseboro 1968-69 C

Randy Ruiz 2008 1B

Jason Ryan 1999-2000 RHP

Michael Ryan 2000-05 OF

S

Ted Sadowski 1961-62 RHP

Mark Salas 1985-87 C

Benj Sampson 1988-89 LHP

Alex Sanchez 1986 OF

Ken Sanders 1973 RHP

Mo Sandford 1995 RHP

Johan Santana 2000-07 LHP

Jack Savage 1990 RHP

Mac Scarce 1978 LHP

Dan Schatzeder 1987-88 LHP

Al Schroll 1961 RHP

Ken Schrom 1983-85 RHP

Ron Schueler 1977 RHP

Erick Schullstrom 1994-95 RHP

Todd Sears 2002-03 1B

Dan Serafini 1996-98 LHP

Gary Serum 1977-79 RHP

John Sevcik 1965 C

John Shave 1998 3B

Jim Shellenback 1977 LHP

Steve Shields 1989 RHP

Garland Shifflett 1964 RHP

Dwight Siebler 1963-67 RHP

Ruben Sierra 2006 DH

Carlos Silva 2004-2007 RHP

Bill Singer 1976 RHP

Kevin Slowey 2007-09 RHP

Roy Smalley 1976-82; 85-87 SS

Mike Smith 2006 RHP

Ray Smith 1981-83 C

Roy Smith 1986-90 RHP

Mike Smithson 1984-87 RHP

John Smiley 1992 LHP

Jim Snyder 1961-62; '64 2B

Eric Soderholm 1971-75 3B

Rick Sofield 1979-81 OF

Paul Sorrento 1979-81 1B

Denard Span 2008-09 OF

Chris Speier 1984 SS

Scott Stahoviak 1993; 1995-98 1B

Kevin Stanfield 1979 RHP

Lee Stange 1961-64 RHP

Randy St. Claire 1979 RHP

Terry Steinbach 1997-99 C

Mike Stenhouse 1995 OF

Buzz Stephen 1968 RHP

Dave Stevens 1994-97 RHP

Shannon Stewart 2003-06 OF

Dick Stigman 1962-65 LHP

Chuck Stobbs 1961 LHP

Les Straker 1987-88 RHP

Jim Strickland 1971-73 LHP

Frank Sullivan 1962-63 RHP

John Sutton 1978 RHP

Anthony Swarzak 2009 RHP

Greg Swindell 1997-98 LHP

T

Kevin Tapani 1989-95 RHP

Jerry Terrell 1973-77 SS

Tim Teufel 1983-85 2B

Bob Tewksbury 1997-98 RHP

Greg Thayer 1978 RHP

Brad Thomas 2001; '03 LHP

George Thomas 1971 OF

Danny Thompson 1970-76 SS

Paul Thormodsgard 1977-79 RHP

Luis Tiant 1970 RHP
Terry Tiffee 2004-06 3B
Tom Tischinski 1969-71 C
Matt Tolbert 2008-09 IF
Fred Toliver 1988-89 RHP
Kelvin Torve 1988 1B
Cesar Tovar 1965-72 OF, IF
Mike Trombley 1992-99; 2002 RHP
George Tsamis 1993 LHP
Lee Tunnell 1989 RHP
Bill Tuttle 1961-63 OF
Jason Tyner 2005-07 OF

U
Ted Uhlaender 1965-67 OF
Scott Ullger 1983 1B

V
Sandy Valdespino 1965-67 OF
Jose Valdivielso 1961 SS
Javier Valentin 1997-99; 2002 C
Elmer Valo 1961 OF
Jesus Vega 1979-80; '82 1B
John Verhoeven 1980-81 RHP
Zoilo Versalles 1961-67 SS
Bob Veselic 1980-81 RHP
Frank Viola 1982-89 LHP

W
Matt Walbeck 1994-96 C
Todd Walker 1996-2000 2B
Charley Walters 1969 RHP
Mike Walters 1983-84 RHP
Danny Walton 1973; '75 OF
Gary Ward 1979-83 OF

Jay Ward 1963-64 3B
Curt Wardle 1984-85 LHP
Ron Washington 1981-86 IF
Scott Watkins 1995 LHP
Tommy Watkins 2007-08 IF
Gary Wayne 1989-92 LHP
Lenny Webster 1989-93 C
Bob Wells 1999-2002 RHP
Boomer Wells 1992 1B
Vic Wertz 1963 1B
David West 1989-92 LHP
Pete Whisenant 1961 OF
Bill Whitby 1964 RHP
Rondell White 2006-07 OF
Len Whitehouse 1983-85 LHP
Mark Wiley 1975 RHP
Rob Wilfong 1977-82 2B
Al Williams 1980-84 RHP
Don Williams 1963 RHP
Glenn Williams 2005 3B
Stan Williams 1970-71 RHP
Carl Willis 1991-95 RHP
Tack Wilson 1983 OF
Dave Winfield 1993-94 OF, DH
Jim Winn 1998 RHP
Larry Wolfe 1977-78 3B
Al Woods 1986 OF
Dick Woodson 1969-70;'72-74 RHP
Al Worthington 1964-69 RHP
Butch Wynegar 1972-82 C

X-Y-Z
Richard Yett 1985; 1990 RHP
Delmon Young 2008-09 OF
Geoff Zahn 1977-80 LHP

Jim Hoey, a graduate of Saint Mary's University in Winona, has taught social studies to secondary school students for more than thirty years, leaving much of his summers free to follow the Twins. His passion for Twins baseball started in 1961, when, as an eight-year old, he listened to broadcasts on his grandfather Ambrose's Zenith radio in his hometown of Taconite, Minnesota. He remains as big a fan of the Twins today as he was in those early years on the Mesabi Iron Range, and his passion shines through in this book's vast array of remarkable feats and curious, little-known facts, statistics, records, and awards. Over the years, Jim has attended more than a thousand Twins games, and he numbers these among his favorite Twins moments:

- Celebrating the '87 World Series title on the streets of Minneapolis
- Catching Kirby Puckett's last grand slam
- Attending the Puckett and Winfield Hall of Fame inductions
- Witnessing Rod Carew's flirtation with .400 in 1977
- Rooting for his all-time favorite player, Bert Blyleven
- Listening to any radio broadcast by Herb Carneal
- Witnessing two Twins' triple plays at Fenway on his honeymoon
- Attending home playoff games with his wife, Ann, and son, Eddie
- Watching a game on TV with his dad